Our Homes, Our Lives

Choice in later life living arrangements

Edited by Keith Sumner

GW00808665

Centre for Policy on Ageing
Housing Corporation

First published in 2002
by the Centre for Policy on Ageing
19–23 Ironmonger Row
London EC1V 3QP
Tel: +44 (0)20 7553 6500
Fax: +44 (0)20 7553 6501
Email: cpa@cpa.org.uk
Website: www.cpa.org.uk

Registered charity no 207163
© 2002 Centre for Policy on Ageing and the Housing Corporation

British Library Cataloguing in Publication Data
A catalogue record for this book is available from the British Library

ISBN 1 901097 85 4

Cover design by Roger Daniels
Typeset by M Rules
Printed in the United Kingdom by Henry Ling Limited,
at the Dorset Press, Dorchester, DT1 1HD

'The potentialities of older people for themselves and for the rest of society have got to find expression'

Peter Laslett, 1989 – from *A Fresh Map of Life*

Peter Laslett b. 1915 – d. 2001

Contents

Foreword

The level of public and political debate on most issues affecting older people in our society is, on the whole, sadly inadequately informed and often trivialised. Too often older people are discussed in terms of a problem population presenting a threatening economic burden to current and future generations. They are also often talked about as if they are members of the same homogenous group, bound together, above all, by the number of years they carry. Little acknowledgement is made as to their considerable diversity, unlike that which is reflected in the portrayal of our younger citizens. The different levels of wealth and poverty; the range of cultural aspirations and practice; the variations in health and frailty, these all influence the way in which different needs and wishes of older people are manifested. How society responds is a different matter.

Public policy in all its spheres is affected by fashion swings, and these in turn can result in reductionist sloganising. The impact on practice and exercise of choice where older people are concerned can be seen in phrases such as 'staying put' or 'going into care' stripped of any context or qualification, but adopted uncritically by politicians and professionals. We can see how these simplified approaches make it harder for older people and their families to achieve the happier, healthier and more fulfilling lives that they have a right to enjoy and to which we all aspire.

The importance of the programme of seminars set up by the Centre for Policy on Ageing, and which form the basis of this book, lies in the way the contributors have opened up the debate and have put back into it many necessary insights and arguments. They help by showing how many choices there are in the spectrum of different living arrangements both in the UK and abroad. They have explored the meaning of words in everyday use such as 'independence' and 'choice' and they have challenged a great deal of conventional wisdom. Part of the success of the seminars was due to the mixture of people who came together to contribute to them. They included academics, housing, health and social care professionals, representatives of voluntary and private sector agencies. Most crucially, at all times, there were those who themselves were older people, either as individuals who spoke on their own behalf or as representatives of Better Government for Older People, or retirement community residents' committees, for example. The papers, which are published here, show the range of expertise and experience across disciplines and organisational cultures, this cross fertilisation also characterised the seminar discussions following the formal presentations.

Among the values which we attach to living a life of quality in old age 'independence' and 'autonomy' rank among the most important. People may not actually use these terms, but their meaning is widely shared. Where the issues of independence and autonomy were examined in the seminars, it became clear how they can be interpreted in very different settings. For example, you do not have to be living in the home you have been in for most of your adult life to enjoy some kind of independence. However, if you are living in someone else's home, or in a residential care home, then the degree to which independence can be felt will rely upon the sensitivity and ethos of those who run and staff the home. Everyday living routines must enable choices to be made about personal surroundings, food, visitors and activities, to name just a few. All of these aspects have been covered at length in numerous codes of practice, official guidance and statutory regulation. In spite of this, practice remains inconsistent. In the best, and probably the majority, of Homes, the concepts of choice, privacy and autonomy are encouraged and applied, in some, appearances are not matched by practice. Conversely, people can remain in their own homes, trapped by infirmity, isolated and at risk from falls. In such cases, the concept of independence loses its primacy, and realities of loneliness or insecurity loom larger. These contrasting circumstances surely point out some of the problems in equating 'independence' with 'staying put' and loss of independence with entering into some form of specialised accommodation or care home.

The seminars have showed how it is possible to escape from this false dichotomy by exploring other options for living arrangements. Accommodation commonly referred to as 'sheltered housing' is a diverse and changing sector of provision, significantly different these days from the old and increasingly hard-to-let local authority sheltered housing schemes. Today there is a wider range of provision in this sector, and many housing associations (Registered Social Landlords) and private developments have moved ahead with far higher spatial standards than hitherto. The implications of the Government's 'Supporting People' policies will also have an impact upon the way in which older residents care needs are met in such housing schemes.

Co-housing, the subject of one of the seminars, is one of the most exciting possibilities being opened up. Though still very underdeveloped in the UK, the Netherlands offers some intriguing examples of different co-housing schemes in operation. These seem to enshrine the concepts of choice and mutuality in a way that few other options have achieved. Here, residents have made a careful and considered choice about the kind of life they wish to lead, and the kind of people they wish to share it with. They have agreed to a way of life and have been accepted by their fellow residents. At the same time, family links, where they exist, are maintained; there is space for visitors to stay, and time and space for privacy and independence. In this sense, it is not a commune or communal living as it used to be understood. Shared interests and experience make for cohesion, and I believe there needs to be much more discussion about the importance of this aspect in planning services.

We hear repeatedly, and we know from our own experience, how expectations have risen about our housing over the past thirty years or so. Things, which were considered luxuries in the 1970s, are now seen as both attainable and necessary. Older people are far less likely to accept that their increasing years mean a scaling down of comfort and reduction of everyday amenities. Sadly, the area where this is most likely to be felt is in long term care, in particular as far as spatial standards are concerned. The contrast between the models of supported housing, co-housing, retirement villages and so on and the residential and nursing home sectors in terms of space, with all that this entails, was striking. The reasons are not hard to understand. Newly built schemes for long term care can and do take account of people's rising expectations, but older homes are in many cases not adaptable enough, nor in a position to afford the necessary changes.

There are, however, many excellent examples of good design where there is a clear 'fit' between the needs and daily living patterns of older residents and the design of the physical environment. The annual UCB Care Homes Design Awards scheme run until recently to identify such good practice was a valuable way of showing what is possible. More and more architects are taking an active interest in the area of specialist living arrangements for older people and seeking their views in the process.

Choice in living arrangements has been the title and the recurring theme throughout the series of seminars. A vista of choices opened up as the discussion went on. The questions that persisted in coming alongside, centred on the reality of choice in the everyday world. For some, choice can only be exercised if it is accompanied by a degree of economic power. For others, the exercise of choice requires a basis of full information. This is possibly a more serious issue, as without the necessary information for older people and their families to make an informed decision, access to the different options remains difficult. Part of the problem is surely the way in which housing and housing issues have been detached at policy and at resource levels from health and social care issues. Until these can be brought into the same governmental mindset, 'Supporting People' not withstanding, access to different forms of living arrangements may remain tantalisingly hard to reach.

That is part of the value of this book – that it may inform those in a position to open up the paths of choice by widening the debate at policy making levels, both nationally and locally. The well-documented demographic forecasts about the increasing number of very old people in Britain over the next fifty years, Professor Tom Kirkwood's Reith Lectures in 2001 on patterns of ageing (or non-ageing), the implications of demands on the NHS, if all taken together, may reinforce the perception of old people as a major societal problem. What this book offers is a very positive approach to counter this view, one of older people taking decisions about their own lives and the places in which they want to live them. Our debt to the Centre for Policy on Ageing and to Keith Sumner who organised and orchestrated this series of seminars is considerable. So too is that to the contributors who have given so much.

Kina, Lady Avebury

Acknowledgements

On 17 July 2001 the Centre for Policy on Ageing (CPA) held the first of its seminars in the 'Choice In Later Life Living Arrangements' series. This and the five seminars which were to follow, a national conference and the preparation of the book, have occupied over a year and a half of my time at CPA.

From the outset it was felt important that the issues raised and the debates entered into should be disseminated to a much wider audience than the seminar format would allow. The production of the book has been a shared experience, it would not have been possible without the generosity of those whose work is reproduced here and who contributed so much to the success of the seminars in which they were involved. CPA was very fortunate to receive the support of the Housing Corporation for the seminar series and the national conference, and also this publication as part of their Improving Practice Grants Programme.

In addition to the authors, I would like to thank Kina, Lady Avebury, Professor Mim Bernard and Nigel Appleton. All of who have acted as Chair for seminars during the series. Also, Maria Brenton, Professor Roger Clough, Dr Gillian Dalley, Leonie Kellaher and Dr Sheila Peace. Each made an exceptional commitment to the success of the series, acting as presenters, discussants and participants over the twelve-month period for which it ran. Their presence provided a thread of consistency amongst the changing groups of participants and was invaluable in opening up the exploration of issues during the free discussion sessions.

I would also like to thank all those individuals who took part in the series and shared openly, their experiences, thoughts and beliefs, some one hundred in all.[1] They provided us with such rich and varied material, I hope that some of the flavour of this is reflected in the book.

Finally, I would like to thank my colleagues at CPA who have helped to bring this book into being in a variety of ways, from assisting with the smooth running of the seminars to the myriad editorial, design and production tasks. In particular, Gillian Dalley, Trish Harwood and Angela Clark.

Keith Sumner
June 2002

---

[1] A full list of participants is provided in the Appendix.

About the contributors

Professor Isobel Allen is Emeritus Professor of Health and Social Policy at the Policy Studies Institute. She has research interests across a broad spectrum of areas including: the interface between health and social care; health care of homeless people; community care; residential care of older people.

Kina, Lady Avebury is Vice Chair of the Board of Governors at the Centre for Policy on Ageing, London. She was Chair of the advisory groups responsible for compiling the residential codes of good practice *'Home Life'* and *'A Better Home Life'* (CPA 1984, 1996).

Maria Brenton is a Visiting Research Fellow, School for Policy Studies, University of Bristol. Currently she is consultant to the 'Older Womens' CoHousing Group', funded by the Joseph Rowntree Foundation, to assist the group in establishing a co-housing community in London.

Dr Vanessa Burholt is Deputy Director, Centre for Social Policy Research and Development, University of Wales, Bangor. She is also a Research Fellow for Training, North Wales Research and Development Support Service, and the Development Officer for Postgraduate Gerontology Studies. Her background is in sociology and psychology.

Professor Roger Clough is Professor of Social Care, Department of Applied Social Science, University of Lancaster. Before his academic work his background was within the field of social care and local government with periods as a Chief Inspector for Social Services, in residential social work and social work teaching.

Dr Gillian Dalley is Director of the Centre for Policy on Ageing. Before joining the Centre she was a senior manager in the NHS, working for a regional health authority and a researcher at the Policy Studies Institute. Her academic training is in anthropology.

Robin Darton is a Research Fellow at the Personal Social Services Research Unit (PSSRU), University of Kent. He been with PSSRU since 1979 specialising in research into long term care for older people, statistical information systems for long term care, and methodological issues relating to the design and analysis of surveys and experiments.

Malcolm Fisk is the Director of Insight Social Research Ltd. He is also a Research Associate at the Centre for Social Research, Queens University, Belfast. His expertise and research interests are concerned with the interface of housing and care, also the role of 'smart technology' in promoting independence in later life.

Kalyani Gandhi is Executive Director of the Eastwards Trust Housing Association. Eastwards Trust provide a range of accommodation including supported accommodation for older people and those with a disability. They cater for the South Asian communities in and around London

Dr Karen Glaser is a Lecturer in Gerontology at the Age Concern Institute of Gerontology, King's College, London. Her research interests include: the living arrangements of older people in Great Britain and changes in residence patterns over time; comparisons in co-residence, kin availability, proximity, and the provision of care for older people between Great Britain and Southern Europe.

Professor Julienne Hanson, Faculty of the Built Environment, University College London is also the Director of the Space Syntax Laboratory at the Bartlett School of Graduate Studies, UCL. She has recently been involved with the ESPRC EQUAL project, profiling the UK housing stock for older people.

Helena Herklots is the Assistant Director, Head of Policy, Age Concern England. She leads the policy unit and is involved in numerous publications and campaigns run by Age Concern England within the field of ageing, to enhance the quality of life of older people.

Leonie Kellaher is Director, Centre for Environmental and Social Studies in Ageing, University of North London. Recent research undertakings include a study of residential care home occupants perceptions of their lives 'in care' for the Centre for Policy on Ageing, an ESRC project on 'Cemetery as Garden' and an ESPRC EQUAL project looking at spatial arrangements in housing for older people.

Steve Ongeri is a Senior Policy Analyst at the Housing Corporation. He has a specialist role in policy development for older people and people with a disability. He is also involved in policy work for rural housing issues, rents, geographical data, and welfare benefits.

Dr Sheila Peace is a Senior Lecturer at the School of Health and Social Welfare, the Open University. Her research interests span many aspects of residential care services, including regulation and care regimes. She also has an interest in environments and ageing.

Keith Sumner is a Policy Officer at the Centre for Policy on Ageing. His academic training is in social gerontology and social work, where he held a number of senior practice and management posts within local authority social services departments. His research interests span the health and social care fields, particularly at the interface.

Dr Cecilia Tomassini is a Research Associate at the Age Concern Institute of Gerontology, Kings College, London. She is also a researcher at the Department of Demography, University La Sapienza, Rome. Her fields of interest include family and social network at old ages, and determinants of mortality at old ages.

Judith Torrington is a Lecturer in the School of Architecture, University of Sheffield. She also runs her own practice, specialising in the design of residential buildings for older people. Judith is also a member of the management committee of a voluntary residential care home, and a lay assessor and member of the NHS and Community Care Act Advisory Panel for Derbyshire County Council.

1 Introduction

Keith Sumner

Aims

This book is concerned with setting an agenda to challenge assumptions and 'givens' with regard to our understanding of the wishes and expectations, as well as the needs, of older people as they relate to housing and care.

Two fundamental principles are at the core of the debates contained in the chapters that follow:

- choice and the accommodation of diversity;

- the full and active involvement of older people in all aspects of planning and decision making.

To make choice a reality requires the availability of an adequate range of housing provision, policy support to allow for the diversity of wants and needs of older people and, inevitably, adequate resourcing of the sectors. Any consideration of diversity must encompass gender and ethnicity as well as economic and attitudinal factors. Adequate information systems to inform people of their rights and facilitate opportunities to exercise these rights, is also key.

The involvement of older people as active partners in planning their future living arrangements, and elements of care support, must be at the heart of day-to-day practice, policy planning and design.

The contributors to this book provide us with descriptions of the current situation, in terms of the 'market place', policy issues, architectural and design perspectives and conceptual understandings of autonomy and independence. They also challenge us to view things differently, to question our conventional approach to this area of social policy (and practice), offering fresh perspectives and potential drivers for bringing about change.

The authors are drawn from a range of settings: leading academics and researchers, senior professionals from the housing and social care fields, and senior managers of housing and care provider organisations. This diversity of professional backgrounds gives us a broad range of perspectives and personal styles which contribute to an eclectic and challenging range of papers covering a broad spectrum of topics key to this debate. A common thread throughout the book is a strong commitment to change practices to impact positively on the quality of older people's lives.

The main body of each chapter is followed by a commentary section, in which specific points raised in the paper may be expanded upon or challenged. These contributions also outline for the reader other aspects of these discussions that complement those already raised. In structuring the book in this way, it is intended that some of the flavour of the reciprocal nature of the development of seminar participants understanding, gained during the series that inspired this project, is transferred to this medium.

This book is aimed at a wide readership, and is intended to stimulate the debate as to how this agenda can be taken forward. It is particularly hoped that it will be used as a resource by:

● practitioners, policy makers, and managers in the housing and social care fields to encourage them to question their own organisational and professional practices;

● students of social policy, housing and social care/social work – to raise questions about 'received wisdom' in relation to agency service delivery and planning models; also to challenge conventional assumptions within society, about the role and capacity of older people (and other marginalised groups) to be central to these processes;

● social gerontologists and students of this discipline.

Overview

In chapter 2 Dr Gillian Dalley explores in some detail the changing patterns in living arrangements and expectations of older people, raising important questions about the political and ideological assumptions behind 'promoting independence' and 'staying put'. She examines the question of the reality of 'independence' as it is experienced by older people supported in the community, and questions the pervading perception that residential forms of care are somehow intrinsically incapable of providing not only the safety and security which may be desired, but the privacy, support and continued self-determination so important to an individuals wellbeing.

Leonie Kellaher (chapter 3) considers the meaning of choice for older people. How do older people make choices around accommodation and care? Some impressions of the adequacy of alternatives are provided, as is an analysis of what forms of housing older people occupy. She goes on to offer a fascinating insight into the issue of 'spatial compression' and the use of space by older people as they try to redefine themselves and their lives in a new home. Finally she looks at the assumptions that sustain existing patterns of provision, and speculates as to how this can be re-cast for the future.

Dr Karen Glaser and Dr Cecilia Tomassini (chapter 4) offer a fresh analysis of trends in population ageing with a particular focus on patterns emerging through the 1990s. They examine living arrangements, receipt of care, residential proximity, and housing preferences in the UK, making some revealing comparisons with patterns prevalent in Italy.

In chapter 5 Professor Isobel Allen provides an historical perspective on the extent to which policies in the residential and community care fields, introduced over the last fifteen years, facilitate the realisation of the expectations of older people. A consideration of recent trends in patterns of available support is undertaken, and the point is raised about the dangers in persisting with the current under-valuing of residential forms of care which risks further reducing the availability of this option for those who need (and choose) it.

Maria Brenton introduces us to a discussion on older people choosing and managing their own community (chapter 6) through a detailed consideration of the co-housing model, which has taken root in parts of mainland Europe, particularly the Netherlands. She discusses the underpinning principles of this communal, or co-operative form of living, some of the benefits it brings and the real difficulties of bringing about such a venture in the UK. The work of the London based Older Women's CoHousing group (OWCH) in trying to set up such a community is discussed in some detail.

The final paper is from Professor Julienne Hanson, who examines how architecture impacts on the way living environments are experienced by their inhabitants. She goes on to explore the role of architects and their responsibilities in ensuring that older people, as 'end-users', are beneficiaries of good design that builds in, as far as is possible, those factors known to enhance quality of life for its occupants, not the victims of a lack of consideration and consultation.

A short discussion chapter is included to pull together some of the main elements explored throughout these texts.

To conclude this introductory chapter I shall provide some grounding for the debate which unfolds during the course of the book.

Context

At this time of unprecedented change in both the health and social care sectors, we have reached a pivotal point in the position of many of the forms of accommodation and care that have traditionally been available to older people such as sheltered housing and residential homes. At the same time we are seeing fundamental changes in the make-up, attitudes and living patterns within the older population. A willingness to take on new ideas to address these 'social facts' is essential if policy solutions are to be found to make these aspirations a reality.

The demographic imperative

It is now widely known that for the next twenty to thirty years the demographic characteristics of the population will continue to undergo rapid and increasing change. The age profile is seeing a major growth in those aged 65+ (a rise in the region of 60 per cent between 1995 and 2031), this is even more marked amongst the 85+ group in which there will be an 80 per cent rise over the same period. An additional 1.2 million people of retirement age by 2011 compared with 1998 figures, rising to an additional 1.5 million by 2021.

We are also seeing changes in the patterns of the socio-economic position of older people. Average incomes continue to rise and future cohorts of the 65+ age group will be better off than comparator groups at present. However, we also have rising inequality, the gap between the well off and the poor within this group is expanding. This diversity of financial means is an important factor when discussing choice and housing markets in terms of accessibility in addition to availability.

Major changes in patterns of household tenure and composition are taking place. There are increasing numbers of older owner occupiers (likely to reach 75 per cent of those aged 65+ by 2010). The role of Home Improvement Agencies will become increasingly important in assisting owners to maintain these properties and to remain living there. The availability of flexible and appropriate equity release products is also of significance here.

Within the overall increase in the number of older people, there is a growth in the number of one person households (currently around 15 per cent for those at retirement age, set to rise to 20 per cent by 2021). By far the largest group are women, around twice the number of men living alone in each age cohort. This ratio increases further with age (85+ men 43 per cent, women 72 per cent, ONS 2000). When focussing on sheltered housing alone this skew is even more marked, with 75 per cent of residents living alone, gender imbalances persist.

Around 5 per cent of those aged 65+ live in sheltered housing. The growth in public sector rented housing has declined, as have the numbers of older people choosing this type of accommodation. The 1990s saw significant growth in the independent sector (Peace and Johnson 1998). Privately owned or rented sheltered housing now accounts for around 13 per cent of properties. There is currently a growth in the provision of 'very sheltered' or 'extra care' housing, which accounts for around 3.5 per cent of all sheltered accommodation. At the same time, there is a continuing and increasing difficulty in letting many of the older, smaller one bedroom or bedsit type sheltered properties. This factor, indicative of older people's changing and rising expectations, is supported by the findings of a number of recent studies (Fletcher *et al.* 1999). The aspirations of older people are continuing to move towards those held by the rest of the population (Tinker *et al.* 1995). They are consequently more likely to refuse offers of such accommodation than in the past.

Residential care also provides accommodation for around 5 per cent of the population of those aged 65+. This sector has changed greatly over the last twenty years, with a major shift from a public sector domination of provision up to the early 1980s, to around 78 per cent of provision now being located in the independent and voluntary sectors (Laing & Buisson 1998). Though local authorities are still the major purchasers of residential care places, a significant proportion of this population continue to elect to move to this form of provision and fund themselves (around 28 per cent). Those qualifying for 'Preserved Rights' account for around 22 per cent (Oldman 1998), funding for this group became a local authority responsibility during 2002.

With increased regulation and scrutiny from the mid-1980s onwards, quality standards have risen, albeit from a low base and inconsistently. The forms that residential provision now takes are quite diverse in terms of size, care regimes, communities of interest, etc. Recent years have seen transformations in the mix of providers in terms of locally run independent homes (often as family businesses) and large regional or national businesses moving into this sector, though this 1990s trend has slowed down.

Pickard *et al.* (2000) predict an increase of 45 per cent in the numbers of 'dependent' older people living alone by 2031 compared with 1996 numbers (i.e. those requiring help with domestic or personal care tasks as defined in the General Household Survey 1994/95). Computer modelling is used to identify a predicted 88 per cent growth in the number of older people aged 85+ likely to need long term care during the same period. This has inevitable implications for both the planning of housing and care services.

Policy framework

It is widely accepted that 'staying put' and traditional conceptions of 'family-based' models of care are the most desirable options for all older people (Dalley 1993). For the last twenty years government policy formulation has been driven by this belief, arguing that this option reflects peoples wants and should take primacy. Recent support for this is demonstrated by three key developments:

- the NHS and Community Care Act (1990) that aimed to

contain the residential care budget by giving social services departments a gate-keeping role through assessment for eligibility. This fostered the growth of the home care sector and the resourcing of Home Improvement Agencies;

- the 1998 provision of the Promoting Independence Special Grants to local authorities, that tied funding to promoting independence at home, rehabilitation and introducing preventative services and support for carers;

- additional funding in 2000 for Intermediate Care Schemes enabled another significant step down this path.

The largely negative associations which research has equated with the consequences of communal forms of living adopted by most residential and nursing care homes has, recently, become more muted, ambivalence on the part of government, wider society and the majority of the research community has emerged. There is a tension between the rejection of 'institutional' forms of care and a tacit acceptance that they continue to fulfil a role not addressed by alternative models of provision.

The recent publication of the housing strategy for older people, *Quality and Choice for Older People's Housing: a strategic framework* (DETR/DH 2001), continues to drive the 'staying put' agenda forward. Despite stating that choice and diversity of provision are required if older people's needs are to be met, that the present situation falls well short of this and that practice acceptable in the past is no longer so, it fails to go on and explore the policy implications of this position. The strategy also reveals ambivalence towards 'extra care' housing asserting that it is not a panacea and questioning the wisdom of combining accommodation and care in a built form.

A positive role for residential forms of care, as part of this spectrum, has been almost entirely neglected, though a public and private sector role in terms of accommodation with care, and support for those with specialist care needs such as dementia, is briefly acknowledged. This position is at odds with sections of the document that stress the need to adopt a whole systems approach within a Best Value framework and fails to address this very specialised part of the spectrum.

The strategy's focus stays firmly upon mainstream housing provision and raising standards. Its emphasis is on enhancing the potential for 'staying put' through:

- architectural design
- secure funding for Home Improvement Agencies
- disabled facility grants
- promoting equity release mechanisms

It reiterates the commitment to a move away from 'institutional forms of care', emphasising independence achieved through being part of the community. This is both welcome and necessary, but it only addresses part of the current situation for older people.

There is some evidence that whilst the majority of older people clearly wish to remain in their present home or similar mainstream independent housing for as long as possible, others prefer to live in some form of alternative setting or smaller property which would be more manageable (McCafferty 1994, Sykes and Leather 1996). This includes a range of forms of communal living such as private sheltered housing, co-housing and residential care. Provision may take the form of communities of interest such as homes for former teachers, nurses or members of the armed services in addition to religion based communities at one end of the scale or continued growth of entire retirement communities such as Hartrigg Oaks in Yorkshire or Bradely village in Staffordshire at the other. A significant proportion of older people has long chosen and continues to actively choose and fund these options for themselves. If real and positive choice to accommodate the diversity in older people's wishes is to be made available then the range of types of accommodation will need to become more varied. We should provide for the fact that significant numbers of older people may opt for specialist provision of some kind, albeit that they will constitute a minority.

References

Dalley, G (1993) Caring: a legitimate interest of older women, in M Bernard and K Meade (eds) *Women Come of Age*, London: Edward Arnold.

DETR/DH (2001) *Quality and Choice for Older People's Housing: a strategic framework*, London: DETR.

Fletcher, P, Riseborough, M and Humphries, J (1999) *Citizenship and Services in Older Age: the strategic role of very sheltered housing*, Beaconsfield: Housing 21.

Laing & Buisson (1998) *Care of Elderly People – Market Survey* 1998, London: Laing & Buisson.

McCafferty, P (1994) *Living Independently: a study of the housing needs of elderly and disabled people*, Department of the Environment Housing Research Report, London: HMSO.

Oldman, C (1998) *Living in a Home: the experience of living and working in residential care in the 1990s*, Kidlington: Anchor Trust.

ONS (2000) *People Aged 65 and Over*, London: Office for National Statistics.

Peace, S and Johnson, J (1998) Living arrangements of older people, in M Bernard and J Phillips (eds) *The Social Policy of Old Age*, London: Centre for Policy on Ageing.

Pickard, L, Wittenberg, R, Comas-Hererra, A, Davies, B and Darton, R (2000) Relying on informal care in the new century? Informal care for elderly people in England to 2031, *Ageing and Society* 20(6) (November):745–772.

Sykes, R, and Leather, P (1996) *The Future of Community Care: a consumer perspective*, Kidlington: Anchor Trust.

Tinker, A, Wright, F and Zelig, H (1995) *Difficult to Let Sheltered Housing*, London: HMSO.

2 Independence and autonomy – the twin peaks of ideology

Gillian Dalley

Introduction

This paper is in four sections. First, I shall consider the changing profile of older people in terms of their numbers, their increased longevity, their lifestyle and their living arrangements. Then I want to look at an aspect of the current ideology of ageing and its associated norms of residence, which are the types of living arrangements that are favoured within this ideological framework. I shall consider how they impinge on older people and how they have informed policy and practice over the last fifty years. Finally, I want to adopt a different way of looking at what could be available as appropriate living arrangements in older age – a way which tries to step outside the restricted and conformist approach generally adopted. I am deliberately adopting a provocative stance in order to stir up some debate, which is the purpose of this book.

Background

I first want to consider ideology and norms. An anthropologist called Fallers writing in 1961 defined ideology as 'that part of culture which is actively concerned with the establishment and defence of patterns of belief and value' (Fallers 1961). I think it is a useful definition for the purposes of this paper. I want to suggest that the way in which the notion of independence is used to govern all our thinking about old age is ideological. The notion of independence as a pre-eminent principle and virtue, one to be strived for over and above any other, runs through almost all modern policy and practice relating to services for older people and against which all other principles are measured. It takes many shapes – independence can mean 'staying on in one's own home in the face of increasing infirmity'; it can mean 'remaining assertive, self-directed, autonomous, able to make choices – staying in control'. It may also mean 'being self suffi-cient, remaining active and alert'. Independence can also be defined in relation to other people as 'not relying on other people' and 'not being a burden on others' or even as 'standing out from the crowd, not going along with the rest of the herd'. It may also be seen in oppositional relationship as the opposite of being mollycoddled or infantilised and, of course, as the opposite of being dependent. It is through these interpretations of the idea of independence that normative expectations grow – normative expectations about how (and where) people should live in late old age and what is and is not acceptable both to older people themselves and to the policy makers and professionals who dominate their lives. I want to argue that all this is ideolog-ical because the 'rightness' of the principle of independence has become a dominant belief in contemporary culture to which alternative principles are subordinated.

Within this given framework – that is, the idea of independ-ence as a dominating principle – this paper seeks to explore questions that arise in anticipating the onset of infirmity and incapacity in later life and the possible onset of dependency. In doing so it questions the acceptance of the dominance of inde-pendence as the determining factor, suggesting instead that it is only one of a number of factors that may be important. It discusses this against the contemporary picture of what older people do in retirement and in the later stages of life.

The profile of older people at the beginning of the twenty-first century

Most older people live in their own homes but of course this is a value laden statement. 'Own home', using conventional termi-nology, is generally assumed to be 'not living in a communal establishment' (that is a residential or nursing home) nor in shel-tered housing. But it raises the question of people's own perceptions about their 'place of residence'. For the moment I

will use the accepted terminology. At any one time, around 90
per cent of people aged 65 or over live in their own homes. Of
those who do not live in the conventionally described 'own
home', around 5 per cent of people aged 65+ live in residen-
tial/nursing care and a further 5 per cent live in sheltered
housing of some type. The chances of moving into residential
care increase with age so that one in four people over 85 is likely
to move into a care home eventually (Royal Commission on
Long Term Care 1999). The profile of sheltered housing residents
is an ageing one. Since women generally live longer than men,
both residential care and sheltered housing tend to have a female
profile. Women in private sheltered housing outnumber men
substantially. Three quarters of residents in two studies of sheltered housing in 1995 (Rolfe *et al.* 1995) and 1996 (Burns 1996)
were women as compared with only 63 per cent in a study less
than ten years earlier carried out by the Harris Research Centre
(1989). The profile of sheltered owners thus appears to be both
ageing and 'feminising'. It may be worth noting that there is a
widespread ambivalence about the position of sheltered housing
within the housing and care spectrum – should it be regarded as
a person's 'own home' and therefore be regarded as contributing
to the promotion of older people's independence (in line with
government's ideological preference) or should it be regarded as
being a quasi form of institutional living and therefore under-
mining it (Dalley 2001)?

It would be a mistake to think that the 90 per cent of people
who remain in their 'own homes' are necessarily a static group. It
is estimated that the average length of time people stay in one
residence is between five and ten years. A considerable number
of people move in retirement – with peak times for moving just
after retirement and then again at around the age of 80. Indeed,
as far back as 1963, Amelia Harris reported that 30 per cent of
people over 65 had moved within the previous ten years (Harris
1963). People are becoming more adventurous in older age
according to the British Airport Authority, who stated at a Design
Council meeting in June 2001, one in three air travellers is now
over 65 and older people travel more and more and further and
further afield. For many years, people have migrated to the south
coast on retirement and more recently migration to Spain or
other parts of the Mediterranean has become common (King *et
al.* 2000).

This reflects the heterogeneity of older people. Just because people move into the 60+ or 65+ age group, it does not mean that the socio-economic characteristics which they exhibited prior to the transition simply disappear. Differences accrued through life relating to social, educational and economic status, ethnicity, regional and cultural difference remain although they may be less easy to pinpoint – certainly in terms of official classification. However, we do know that there are some major variations within that section of the population over 65 particularly in terms of its demographic and socio-economic characteristics. Much of the variation will increase over the next twenty to thirty years. There will be an increase in the numbers of people living alone, in those who have never married, and those who are childless. There will be a growth in numbers of older people from minority ethnic groups as the first generations of migrants reach retirement age. Patterns of tenure, which have changed over the last thirty years, will continue through the first quarter of this century. Already around two thirds of older people are owner occupiers. It is estimated that this will have risen to over three quarters by 2010 and will continue to rise (DETR/DH 2001). The number of people in receipt of occupational pensions will continue to grow although it will not be a smooth increase. Variable employment experience prior to retirement (reflecting peaks and troughs in unemployment rates during the 1980s and 1990s) will have an impact on pensions entitlement (especially on men). The numbers of women in receipt of occupational pensions will continue to rise. Although older people as a group have steadily become more affluent over the past thirty years, this affluence has not benefited all sections. Indeed a clear polarisation between rich and poor has developed, particularly in recent years. About a quarter of older people are estimated to be living in poverty (defined by income support/minimum income guarantee levels). Some of these will be owner occupiers (property rich/cash poor) but many will be living in some form of social or private rented housing.

Predictions about the state of health of the next generation of older people are generally but guardedly optimistic. The hope is (and this seems to be being borne out by early reports) that along with living longer, people are also more healthy. Rates of limiting long-standing illness in older age seem to be beginning to decline. As the saying goes, 'life is being added to years as well as years to life'. But as with affluence, maintenance of, or improvement in, health status is unlikely to be evenly spread.

The picture then of life in older age is one of variety and dynamism – at least for the majority. But everyone, as the life course progresses, is conscious of the growing possibility – and likelihood – of ill health or frailty setting in. For example, it is estimated that a quarter of those over 85 will develop dementia with one third of them needing constant care or supervision. Depression, sometimes leading to suicide, is more common in people over 65, with some 10–16 per cent being affected (Audit Commission 2000). It is within this context that people begin to think about their future.

Older people's view of future infirmity

People begin to think about the future within a moral context – within a framework of normative expectations and an associated view that the normative practice which flows from them is 'right'. From this, it can be argued, the normative view of infirmity in old age is that, in spite of their infirmity, individuals seek to maintain, achieve or be accorded: independence, autonomy, choice, dignity, privacy, self-esteem, fulfilment. Directly linked to this is a view that suggests these principles or virtues can only be achieved through the individual remaining in her/his own home and that moving into 'an institution' (which may encompass sheltered housing as well as a residential or nursing home) means by definition, and in all cases, a loss of those virtues. Moreover, research is quoted as showing this time and time again. The link between independence as a prime goal and its association with staying in one's own home is made regularly. However, I think it is important to examine the context of that research. There seem to be three factors influencing the way in which 'pro-independence' views are elicited from older people:

1 Stage of life: people are asked about what they want to do in the future at a time when they may be uneasy about contemplating the reality of potential infirmity. Having to answer questions about future living arrangements which are likely to be governed by the onset of infirmity raises the issue of their own mortality. A move into residential care may be seen as confirmation of this.

2 The options which are offered as possible alternatives may be limited in range or be depicted negatively so that residential care is presented as a last resort or as the worst possible option.

3 Value judgements held by the researchers frame the whole project from the outset.

In discussing how much of the research on residential care has focused on its negative aspects (in which loss of independence and loss of one's own home feature large), Oldman and Quilgars (1999) make a telling point about the methodology commonly employed. They say that 'where older people have been consulted, the survey has been the predominant methodology and the questions which have been asked often derive from pre-existing convictions about older people's attitudes and behaviour.' Thus the prevailing negative view of residential care in academic and practice circles conditions the theoretical framework of the research from the outset with outcomes which would favour the residential option tending to be precluded from the start. Two examples:

1 Malcolm Fisk introduces his report for Help the Aged (1999) by asserting that from the earliest days housing and support services have been provided within an ageist framework which has served to foster separation and social exclusion. He regards residential care and sheltered housing as exemplifying this and the substance of the report flows from that starting point.

2 In an abstract for a paper presented at the recent International Association of Gerontology conference, researchers from Wales, describing the application of vignettes as part of their study on housing options for older people, stated that the vignettes 'were structured in order to fit the personal situation, or perceived future situation of the respondents. Given that we know that most people would respond that they desire to age in place, the key question in the in-depth interviews was *What changes in personal circumstances would force you to consider leaving your home?'* (Burholt *et al.* 2001).

And yet, ironically – and perhaps inadvertently – research also reveals that the 'staying put' option is not always the best. Many older people, particularly women living alone, experience loneliness and isolation. The prevalence of depression is especially high among older age groups. Age Concern produced a report (Boyo 2001) in which the voices of older people were heard poignantly describing this isolation:

When I am alone, I feel as if the room will eat me. I get very worried.

When I am alone I feel a lot of fear. There is no life living alone.

When I am alone it gets very difficult and I feel bewildered.

A survey conducted in 1996 by the Harris Research Centre for Tunstall Telecom found that around three quarters of the older people living independently whom they interviewed felt isolated and had little or no life outside their home. A report for Help the Aged in 2001 (Owen 2001) reported similar experiences among a large proportion of older people living in their own homes. The report suggests that nearly a million people could be in this position. But the solution offered is usually in terms of exhorting service providers to provide more support at home rather than to encourage consideration of alternative options. Fisk, for example, suggests that 'our challenge is to stretch the boundary in order to embrace as many older people as possible within the new frameworks that provide support, ... within people's own homes' (Fisk 1999).

Official discourse – professionals and policy makers

Policy makers and professionals have long subscribed to the view that independence is a prime goal, which can best be achieved by 'staying put'. It is consonant with a whole stream of policy documents going back to the 1970s supporting the development of community care, which itself was based on the premise that it is better to maintain people at home than encourage movement into residential care. Recent policy pronouncements since the Labour government's advent in 1997 have confirmed this commitment. The government white paper, *Modernising Social Services* (DH 1998), the NHS Plan (DH 2000) and the housing strategy for older people, *Quality and Choice for Older People's Housing* (DETR/DH 2001), have all set out the commitment to independence through prevention and support as a basic plank in its overall approach. But there is often a gap between principle and practice.

This gap between principle and practice at the policy level is replicated at practitioner level. Oldman and Quilgars (1999), for example, illuminate it in a study of home care recipients and care home residents and their respective staff with an example of the difference between practitioner and resident perceptions. They quote a member of the care home's staff talking about the 'trauma' of going into care:

> *It's difficult. They can't look out anymore on that tree they planted in the garden fifty years previously. They may not have been able to get out into the garden for some time but that tree symbolised a lot.*

But as Oldman and Quilgars point out, the residents in their study did not see it like that and rarely talked in those terms. Like the residents in a study by Isobel Allen and colleagues (Allen *et al.* 1992) they were much more positive about the circumstances they found themselves in, regarding the decision to move into care realistically and unsentimentally. Furthermore, the static view of the residents expressed by the care assistant certainly does not take into account the fact that many older people do not conform to this stereotype of older people continuing to live in the same place all their lives without ever moving, without ever extending their horizons in an expanding world.

The convergence between policy, research and practice has huge consequences for many older people. It leads to a distortion of what residential care could possibly become. Instead of residential care being one among a number of equal options in living arrangements, within state-supported long term/community care policy, it has become the form of care of last resort. Levels of dependency in care homes have increased and despite the best efforts of many homes to raise standards and improve quality of life through developing a wide range of social activities, the dominant characteristic of many homes is one of inactivity and infirmity. It is a development not unnoticed by residents. Some of the residents interviewed by Leonie Kellaher in *A Choice Well Made* complained about the increase in the number of zimmer frames in the lounges, reflecting their concern that their homes were being occupied by people who were more and more dependent. While they were accepting and supportive of fellow residents who became dependent during the course of their residency, they were much less happy about an admissions policy which meant that only people who were already frail would be admitted (Kellaher 2000). This view is confirmed elsewhere in other homes.

The other side of this coin is that increasingly people are being maintained in their own home, in isolation, with very little social support except for an intensive care package, which provides no more than care for the needs created by frailty but does little to meet the need for companionship and other inter-action. This is done under the banner of 'giving support to enable people to remain independent' – the overriding ideolog-ical goal that I described earlier. It is also a contradiction in terms and stretches the meaning of independence. A further and worrying development is that service providers, because of the cost of providing support as well as the shortage of care staff, may become reliant on smart solutions, replacing human interaction with technological solutions. The danger in this is that the indi-vidual at home becomes more and more cut off from the outside world, more and more isolated.

Some commentators have seen the implications of these trends and argue for some redefinition of goals. Thus 'researchers, policy makers, service providers and the media must broaden their definition of independence to include interde-pendence' (White and Groves 1997). But even so, this does not often include a re-examination of the ideological foundations of what 'independence' means.

Alternatives

This brings me to the central point of my argument. First, I want to suggest that in elevating the principle of independence as the essential virtue to be established and maintained at all cost in late old age, gerontologists and health and social care practi-tioners are misreading the 'lived experience' of many older people. In discussing 'autonomy', a concept close to that of inde-pendence, Becker for example shows how it has become the virtuous expression of American core values irrespective of how meaningful it is for the persons to whom it is applied:

> American values that are based on rational determinism, such as independence, responsibility for oneself and one's health, control over the environment, productivity, and future orien-tation, articulate fundamental American notions about personhood, individual autonomy and the power of thought to shape life course and bodily functioning and constitute an American ideology of individualism. This ethos of independ-ence and autonomy minimizes interdependence.
>
> (Becker 1994)

Pointing out how foreign this position is in other societies (she cites the Hopi), Becker asserts that the degree of importance placed on the notion of autonomy is culture-specific (American for her, but applicable to much of western society in general, I would argue). But for those coping with the onset of infirmity, this aggressive assertion of autonomy may not only be unhelpful to them, it may positively hinder their ability to come to terms with their day-to-day experience and seek other more fruitful solutions to the problems of daily living. The ideas of interdependence, reciprocity and mutuality, for example, find little place in a normative environment conditioned by an individualistic cleaving to ideas of independence and autonomy (Dalley 1996).

If independence were downplayed and these counterbalancing concepts were acknowledged, acceptable options for older people might emerge. People then could reasonably expect to look for:

> companionship and friendship; mutuality; common interest; support and personal care; social activity; the easing of responsibility for daily functioning (house-cleaning, cooking, gardening); freedom from fear of isolation, loneliness and danger.

We already know that these expectations underpin the decisions of many people who have made the move into some sort of supported housing or residential care (Rolfe 1995; Allen *et al.* 1992). We also know that many people confirm that their expectations are met once they have made the move. It is important to recognise that having this set of expectations met does not necessarily preclude the satisfaction of the other aspirations which were mentioned at the start of this piece, that is:

> independence, autonomy, choice, dignity, privacy, self-esteem, fulfilment.

If we remember the isolation which many people experience in staying put, it is arguable that some form of residential care may be better placed to meet at least some of these aspirations than remaining at home alone and incapacitated. But it does run counter to the principle of individualism and the associated notion of sturdy self-reliance both of which underpin the ideology of independence, which has come to dominate social policy relating to older people in the last thirty years.

But this begs the question of what sort of residential care or supported housing can meet these expectations. Clearly all is not well with much residential care as it exists today. We are familiar with cases of authoritarian regimes, homes where there is little stimulation, where residents have almost nothing in common with each other and homes where staff are undertrained and turnover is high. As Roger Clough has pointed out (Clough 1998), residents do not have rights of occupancy or ownership and can have their residency terminated with little notice. It is impossible for the principle of respect for individuals and the according of rights to privacy and choice to be observed in these settings. The idea that residents can exercise control of their circumstances under these conditions and make real choices on both big and little matters in their daily lives is a nonsense.

It is important to remember though that even under current conditions (and we have yet to see what impact the Care Standards Act 2000 will have on raising the quality of residential care in the future) some residential care already meets expectations. Clearly it is important to have variety – the study by Rosemary Bland (1999) contrasting the 'hotel' approach with the 'social care' approach confirms this. Work by Jan Reed and Valerie Payton (1996, 1997) shows that new residents are able to adjust positively to living in a care home – indicating that the building of relationships between residents is more significant than concentrating on the relationship between resident and care staff. Allen *et al.*'s study (1992), which I have already referred to, also found positive adaptations to living in residential care. It is significant that almost all studies mention the importance of choice in helping residents to adapt.

Perhaps most important is that real choice should involve not only the choice of where to live (in one's existing home or in a shared, communal home of some sort), it should also involve choice about *with whom* one lives. Personal satisfaction in large part derives from the building or maintenance of friendship ties and companionship. In a society where marriage has been important, companionship may have been normatively associated with the married couple relationship but in a context of increasing longevity, widowhood and greater solo living, people are likely to seek companionship through other relationships. Thus the idea of communities of attachment, communities of interest based on the idea of mutuality – in which reciprocity and interdependency are important components – become relevant. This is not a new idea. There has been a long history of common interest groups pooling resources and establishing homes for

their older members. A swift count recently came up with the
following examples:

> masons; printers; ex-servicemen of many sorts; Christian
> denominations e.g. Baptist, Methodist, Catholic; many
> different ethnic, cultural, and religion-based groupings, e.g.
> Jewish, Polish, Asian, Chinese; teachers; mineworkers;
> licensed victuallers; police; rail workers; musicians; actors;
> gardeners; women's groups.

Some are long-standing, some have recently come into existence.
They may differ in founding principles but common to all is the
notion that people do not enter late old age free of personal and
cultural 'baggage'. And the 'baggage' they bring with them is
important in enabling themselves to maintain their sense of
identity through the life transitions which they are experiencing
and in enabling them to build new friendship and companionship links in strange new surroundings.

But there are barriers to the development of freely chosen,
freely established ways of coming together in the ways just
described. While the idea of building communities of interest to
offer support and companionship in old age (not just in terms of
bricks and mortar) is an appealing one, it is one which falls foul
of prevailing policy, both ideological and fiscal.

The main obstacle is the ideological opposition to residential
care which runs through all official policy. Using the term generically (in juxtaposition to staying put in one's own home),
residential care is never regarded as an 'open' or 'equal' option as
a form of living arrangements. More than this, as a form of care
it is regarded as the care of last resort and to make matters worse,
ideology is underpinned by the restriction of resources. Thus it
leads to the conflation of what is regarded as 'right' in the ideological sense already described with what is also seen as fiscally
appropriate. All sorts of hurdles to entry are constructed.
Eligibility criteria have been established, which limit admission
to the frailest and most vulnerable in the community. On top of
this, financial assessments linked to the dependency criteria
exclude only the poorest or impose stiff sanctions on those of
moderate means. It is hardly surprising then that it is seen as care
for poor and dependent people – who have signally failed their
biggest test – that is, of being able to remain 'independent' in
their own homes.

Other hurdles also exist. In relation to some types of

supported or communal accommodation, local authority planning and housing rules make it difficult for innovative schemes
catering for community of interest-type schemes to get off the
ground. Local authorities wish to retain rights of tenancy nominations which undermine the idea of a community of interest
arguing that such communities breach the principles of social
housing. (Some of these issues are picked up in later chapters.)
Thus the principle of enabling older people to choose where they
live and with whom is overridden by other concerns (which may
be perfectly valid in other contexts).

The only way official opposition can be contested is through
self-funding. This may be achieved by having enough money to
pay the fees in residential care or by having sufficient capital to
buy into some form of leasehold provision of choice. A situation
has now developed, in traditional residential care homes, of
occupancy being made up of the very poorest and most
dependent on the one hand and those who have private means
with various degrees of dependency on the other – and increasingly with the self funders subsidising local authority supported
residents because of the current crisis in funding. This is hardly a
situation in which companionship and mutuality can easily
develop.

To look objectively at the role which residential care *could*
play, we need to be able to look at choice in living arrangements
as something independent of infirmity – which as we have seen
is what better off people can do. Prevailing official antipathy
however makes this impossible.

It would involve investigating more carefully the notion of
'home' and what it means to people as they age. How far is it
associated with the bricks and mortar? How far is it linked to
locality and the community in which it is placed? Does it stand
as a proxy for relationships – happy, painful and sad? Is it merely
a sentimental notion or is it an economic entity about which an
older person has hard-nosed views – especially in relation to
having to sell it in order to pay for care rather than leave it as part
of an inheritance? How far are attachments to home transferable
to other settings? A study recently conducted by Cherry Russell
has questioned what she calls housing research's 'overly roman-
ticised view of the home as the core of an older person's identity'
(Russell 2001). In talking to sixty-six older home dwellers in
Sydney, Australia she found that while attachment to the notion
of home was strong for many of them, it was by no means

universal. She concluded that there was indeed 'considerable diversity in the centrality of home to the construction of personal meaning and identity in later life' and warned policy makers against making unwarranted assumptions about its place in people's lives.

From a contrasting perspective, researchers in Canada (Kontos and Angus 2001) have suggested that with the delivery of long term care directly into people's homes under home care schemes, the nature of 'home' is being changed fundamentally – from traditional notions of home into sites for the labour intensive work of health care professionals and paraprofessionals. The idea that home, as we are encouraged to understand it, can be maintained under these conditions is shown to be compromised severely.

We need perhaps to consider the role of residential care as part of a broad preventive strategy. Despite early optimism in the 1980s that community care (through the introduction of care management and care packages) would prove cheaper than the residential option, this has not been the case. In a broad based housing, home and care strategy, it might be possible to see residential care (defined generically to include all forms of communally supported living) as a preventive measure designed to maintain people's capacity, to enhance their social lives, to build their self-esteem, to protect them and to support them sensitively in the later stages of life. But this would mean an end to the polarisation of attitudes about 'staying put' on the one hand and 'moving on' on the other.

Conclusion: new arrangements for new times

It is important to see that the deficiencies of residential care on the one hand and the pitiful plight of many people living in their own homes on the other say more about the situation of older people in society today than they do about the intrinsic merits of one form of care over the other. The fact that older people also have to pay for these unsatisfactory solutions to their situations is also testament to this.

Older people do not constitute a homogeneous population. They have many and varied needs and many and varied views about how these can be met. We need to take the question of choice and diversity seriously. This means accepting that for some people, the wish to live with like-minded others in what might otherwise be regarded as segregated or excluding settings should be acknowledged. Choice should not be limited only to those options countenanced by current ideological preferences. When Fisk suggests that 'our challenge is to stretch the boundary in order to embrace as many older people as possible within the new frameworks that provide support', he still seems to be excluding the option that I have been arguing for namely that of accepting that for some people – both infirm and able – the preference may be to live together. In doing so he is excluding a significant minority (that is, those who are too helpless and vulnerable to stay put with however much support). They will be labelled as a 'failing' group and be condemned to an even more stigmatised future than ever before as a result of the hegemonic advance of the ideology of independence. The time is ripe, I would argue, for some radical rethinking.

References

Allen, I, Hogg, D and Peace, S (1992) *Elderly People: choice, participation and satisfaction*, London: PSI.

Audit Commission (2000) *Forget Me Not: mental health services for older people*, London: Audit Commission.

Becker, G (1994) The oldest old: autonomy in the face of frailty, *Journal of Aging Studies* 8(1).

Bland, R (1999) Independence, privacy and risk – two contrasting approaches to residential care for older people, *Ageing and Society* 19(5).

Boyo, S (2001) *When a House is Not a Home: older people and their housing*, London: Age Concern England.

Burholt, V et al. (2001) Housing for an aging population: planning implications. Paper presented to the International Association of Gerontology conference, *Gerontology* 47 (S1/01).

Burns, A (1996) *Car Parking for Sheltered Housing*, Bournemouth: McCarthy & Stone.

Clough, R (1998) *Living in Someone Else's Home*, London: Counsel and Care.

Dalley, G (1996) *Ideologies of Caring: rethinking community and collectivism*, Houndsmill: Macmillan.

Dalley, G (2001) *Owning Independence in Retirement: the role and benefits of private sheltered housing*, London: CPA.

DETR/DH (2001) *Quality and Choice for Older People's Housing: a strategic framework*, London: Department of the Environment, Transport and the Regions.

DH (Department of Health) (2000) *The NHS Plan: a plan for investment, a plan for reform*, London: The Stationery Office.

DH (Department of Health) (1998) *Modernising Social Services: promoting independence, improving protection, raising standards*, London: The Stationery Office.

Fallers, LA (1961) Ideology and culture in Uganda nationalism, *American Anthropologist* 63(19).

Fisk, M and Abbot, S (1998) Older people and the meaning of independence, *Generations Review* 8(2).

Fisk, M (1999) *Our Future Home: housing and the inclusion of older people in 2025*, London: Help the Aged.

Harris, A (1963) *Moving House by Elderly People* [reprinted from: Labour mobility in Great Britain, 1953-63, Government Social Survey], GSS SS333.

Harris Research Centre (1989) *A Survey on Sheltered Housing for the Elderly: the facts and the future*, Bournemouth: McCarthy & Stone.

Kellaher, L (2000) *A Choice Well Made: mutuality as a governing principle in residential care*, London: CPA/Methodist Homes.

King, R, Warnes, T and Williams, A (2000) *Sunset Lives: British retirement migration to the Mediterranean*, Oxford: Berg.

Kontos, PC and Angus, J (2001) Home as a site for long term care. Paper presented to the International Association of Gerontology conference, *Gerontology* 47(S1/01).

Oldman, C and Quilgars, D (1999) The last resort? Revisiting ideas about older people's living arrangements, *Ageing and Society* 19(3).

Owen, T/Help the Aged (2001) The high cost of isolation, *Working with Older People* 5(1).

Reed, J and Payton, VR (1996) Constructing familiarity and managing the self, *Ageing and Society* 16(5).

Reed, J and Payton, VR (1997) Understanding the dynamics of life in care homes for older people – implications for de-institutionalizing practice, *Health and Social Care in the Community* 5(4).

Rolfe, S, Mackintosh, S and Leather, P (1995) *Retirement Housing: ownership and independence*, Kidlington: Anchor Housing Association.

Royal Commission on Long Term Care (1999) *With Respect to Old Age. Report of the Royal Commission on the Funding of Long Term Care for the Elderly*, London: The Stationery Office.

Russell, C (2001) Gender, identity and the home in later life. Paper presented to the International Association of Gerontology conference, *Gerontology* 47(S1/01).

Tunstall Telecom Ltd (1996) *Home Alone '97 – Independence and Isolation: life for the over-sixties in today's Britain*, Whitley Bridge: Tunstall Telecom

White, AM and Groves, MA (1997) Interdependence and the aged stereotype, *Australian Journal on Ageing* 16(2).

COMMENTARY 1
Leonie Kellaher

This book is concerned with new attitudes, new times and new worlds. Gillian Dalley's paper gives us an account and an analysis which pushes for radical thinking about age and residence. This response is offered from the perspective of a researcher, until rather recently sceptical of residential care and the possibility of it offering a very positive experience for older people. In considering Gillian's paper I have been struck by a number of issues and questions which may take us a little further in thinking about the case for new dispositions, which may lead to new actions on the part of policy makers, practitioners and older people themselves.

I shall raise a series of discrete points, which may add to the quite substantial argument already put forward by Gillian Dalley. A couple of preliminary points need to be made:

1 If the prevailing ideology of ageing is constructed using notions of independence and autonomy, then we should not be at all surprised to see this ideology made manifest – perhaps even writ large – very large – in patterns of residence and co-residence. Indeed, this is probably the first place we should look. The house, the home, is certainly culturally central, along with family, since it also entails and expresses economic and associative life (or its absence) and gives clues as to the beliefs and values of its inhabitants. There are many stucturalist and material culturalist writers – sociologists and anthropologists – who argue this. Which leads me to a second preliminary point:

2 Analysis of an ideology is a necessary, but perhaps not sufficient, condition for a move towards new attitudes and new dispositions to action. This is what my response aims to achieve. We also need to consider the extent to which my point about the centrality of the house, the home, in cultural constructions, means that we can read off from residence arrangements something about the rules that have come to shape the preferred cultural patterns of living arrangements

Can we say what these 'domestic' rules actually are? If so, do they lead us towards an idea of 'homeness' and, beyond this, can they give clues as to how essential 'homeness' may be and, if so, whether it can be transposed or replicated in new living arrangements? Drawing upon recent and current research about the ordinary, domestic setting rather than the special, residential setting, I have picked up on a couple of points which seem relevant to our discussion.

1 The house or home is a closed unit, economically at least, accommodating the immediate two generational family. Borrowing and lending beyond the boundaries is likely to be very restricted. For example, borrowing or lending a cup of sugar would be very unusual nowadays and judged deviant in many communities. Here we might be reminded of Foucault when he says that 'discipline is a series of anonymous power processes by which people are judged normal or deviating' and, moreover, he argues that these processes are to be detected at the level of detail (1977).

2 What goes on in the home is secret and private. For older people dependence, through different kinds of infirmity and frailty can – up to a point – be kept secret. As a researcher I have, in the past, argued that the residential home setting no longer permits the presentation of a self that is competent. Frailty is revealed, indeed it is the currency and the conduit by which care – albeit in rather restricted quantities – is accessed and delivered. The familiar home, certainly at the micro-level, supports the older person as they negotiate the unfamiliarities of new frailties. This case for familiarity was employed in a recommendation of the 'residential flat-let' model in *A Balanced Life* (Peace *et al.* 1982). Secondly, can we understand anything about the provenance of the rules? Which or who are the parties to their establishment, maintenance and elaboration? Particularly, where are older people themselves in all of this?

I do not think we can be sentimental and say older people play no part in this, collusion occurs, but this is a response to a dominant ideology. They also resist, but quietly. I would argue that post-retirement moving strategies are likely to become increasingly conservative and yet, paradoxically, great risk-taking is attached to making a move in advanced years. To elaborate: whilst we all know that only a minority of older people ever move to an institutional setting (although a substantial minority of those are in their eighties), I have argued that the shadow cast is a long one which frames many, if not all, the decisions about moving or staying put. Many older people weigh up whether, and when, a move is necessary to re-balance the shifting relationship between the built and social environment which constitutes home and their ageing, changing, self.

They do this – arguably – with the image of residential care at the end of the line, something to be avoided at all costs.

This might mean making a precautionary move before it is strictly necessary, before the garden, house and managing become so overwhelming that the residual residential option is all that remains. Generally speaking, social considerations appear to override spatial and geographical ones. The older person making a move, seeks to place themselves, as far as possible, at the centre of a social network. This is the case whether or not their existing network is an extensive or a very limited one. The gain sought is primarily social, though the physical and material are implicated almost equally. Often family relationships are to be maintained – as a consequence of a move – at some level short of the burdensome. Excessive dependence is to be circumvented and a modified version of autonomy to be constructed through a move.

The day-to-day lives of older people in their domestic settings are much more complex than the 'experts' (planners and policy makers) allow for in their guidance, but this, along with concealment of infirmity, is secret. They both engage and disengage, collude and quietly, individually, resist.

We need to ask ourselves, how do ideas of structured dependency fit alongside the ideology of independence and autonomy? The answer is perfectly. Structured dependency defines the limits of independence and forms the two categories. I will return to the question of categories in a moment when I talk about research and methodologies.

Independence is, thus, striven for. It is not to be sacrificed – or even compromised – in the very public arena which is understood as 'traditional' residential care, though this is less clear in hospital and nursing home settings where meanings are less ambiguous and based on the medical model. I have argued in *Re-evaluating Residential Care* (1997), that older people fear the loss of self, entailed in a move to a residential home. The fit self will become obscured as the frail older person is made more and more visible. Essentially, the secluded domestic dwelling is thought to protect against this exposure and, thus, the aspiration to resist residential care has a rationality which cannot be denied.

Without wishing to take a Darwinian stance or evoking too strongly Desmond Morris, I tentatively raise the question as to how far independence might be an evolutionary drive. Which is not to say, as with all such drives, that it has not been culturally harnessed and shaped, and that it could not be re-shaped. I do not have an answer but believe we should at least have the question before us.

The demographic changes, which are ageing western society, seem to hold out the possibility of such re-shaping to accommodate ideas of dependence, perhaps expressed as interdependence. But we have yet to gain experience of a large segment of the population being old, with increased levels of frailty. It may be that the generation ageing now, being healthier and to some degree richer than preceding generations, will resist – perhaps revolt – in different ways against the prescribed arrangements for living. Though I have to confess to a high degree of scepticism, in the past, when policy makers and practitioners, notably not older people themselves, have said that objections to the restrictions of residential care would increase as a more assertive generation graduates to these settings. I have always thought, however, that the structures which have framed residential care are too strong for that.

The 'rules' about living arrangements are generally expressed in categorical terms, which is to say that the continuities and fluctuations which constitute living count for little, if anything, when policy makers, practitioners and researchers approach the topic. We might talk about spectrums or kaleidoscopes of care, hoping to represent the continuities, but the representations of residence and care with which our culture concerns itself appear in highly segmented forms. We have only to consider the current difficulties arising from the categories of personal versus nursing care to remind ourselves of independence sharply delineated from dependence, with ordinary help being located in another sphere to the special one which contains care. To this we might add special and ordinary housing. Re-shaping the options will not rest on re-labelling. Personally I am already suspicious of the term 'lifetime home', inclusive though it sounds, since it seems to be dominated by intrusive designed solutions rather than a simple regulated backdrop to the older person's agency – with help – at home. There is a real problem here, and as a researcher I do not have an easy answer except to say that methods need to be much more amenable to representation of the continuities and complexities of life at home in advanced years.

To conclude, I accept the notion of ideology as that part of culture actively concerned with the establishment and defence of patterns of belief and values, but I would like to add another clause, 'Culture is made up of contagious ideas', and 'that to explain culture is to explain how some ideas happen to be contagious' Sperber (1998, p. 77). If we are to move towards the new attitudes or dispositions required to take a fresh look at forms of living arrangements we have hitherto castigated or represented as stigmatising, do we not also need to understand and tackle the spread of the idea that some forms of living arrangement are stigmatising?

References

Foucault, M (1977) *Discipline and Punish: the birth of the prison*, trans. Alan Sherridan, London: Allen Lane.
Peace, S, Kellaher, L and Willcocks, D (1982) *A Balanced Life?: a consumer study of residential life in a hundred local authority old people's homes*, London: Social Survey Research Unit, Polytechnic of North London.
Peace, S, Kellaher, L and Willcocks, D (1997) *Re-evaluating Residential Care*, Buckingham: Open University Press.
Sperber, D (1996) *Explaining Culture: a naturalistic approach*, Oxford: Blackwell.

COMMENTARY 2
Roger Clough

The debate on independence and autonomy is immensely important because these dominant ideas not only set the parameters for policy but influence individuals' perceptions of their own ageing.

Policy. Each new policy is justified on the basis of promotion of independence. This overarching construction determines the direction of policy and the components of policy. The construction in turn impacts on people who apply for funding (in that applications must be couched in terms of support for independence) and in assessments of the competence of current practice.

Individuals' perceptions. It is tempting to think that people construct their own views of themselves and their worlds. In fact all of us are influenced in assessing our own lives by dominant ideas and therefore it becomes imperative to become aware of the dominant ideas and then to examine their validity.

A key theme is the construction of ageing and of person-hood:

● What are we driven by and what are we pulled towards?

● From where do the dominant ideas come?

● What is the impact of structural constructions of ageing?

Indicators. One strand in the history of the paramount position of independence has been the attempt to find indicators of good and bad welfare practice. There is a long history in which I and others have been involved in trying to look at the acceptability of welfare practices in terms of an examination of their perform-ance against set factors (Booth 1985, Clough 1981, Tizard *et al.* 1975, Willcocks *et al.* 1987). There are several key points:

a) The source of the factors chosen must be examined: whose ideas are they? What degree of importance is – or should be – attached to them?

b) To what extent are the factors indicators, or surrogates? If so, what is the essence that they were striving to identify?

c) How precise is the language that is adopted? To what extent is there a shared meaning for the term?

In part, many of the factors chosen to assess services have been selected because either there would be debates as to the end of services or because the end is difficult to quantify and examine. Thus, factors such as choice should be seen as indicators of some-thing larger, not as ends in themselves. Their relevance is that without the potential for choice the individual can play no part in the services or lifestyle. The paradox becomes clear when it is realised that a large choice is no measure of good services. The same is true, of course, for other descriptors such as privacy. They may come to be seen as absolutes when they are not. You can be private in a prison.

So it becomes important to attempt to understand both the history and the meanings ascribed to two of the terms which are the subject of the paper under discussion: independence and autonomy. In different ways, both are used to try to assert the importance of the individual in negotiations, though empha-sising different elements. Autonomy I take to be akin to a factor I termed 'control of lifestyle' in *Old Age Homes*.

> Control of life-style examines the situation from the point of view of the resident and charts the extent to which the resident has mastery of her own life.
>
> (Clough 1981, pp. 31–2)

Though today I would change the word 'mastery' I would continue to assert the value of looking at the extent to which people can play a part in negotiating both major decisions about their lives (where and with whom to live, for example) and details about their lives (times of meals and bathing). However, in trying to examine life from the perspective of the resident, a major theme of *Old Age Homes*, there is a danger of seeming to demand control by the older person, not their involvement.

The dangers are far greater in terms of the word 'independence'. As with many 'hurrah' words, it may appear difficult to challenge as it seems to be so obviously a good thing. Yet the word has different meanings for different people and demands precision and clarification. There are several components and Wilkin (1989), amongst others, has contributed to unpicking meanings by searching for understanding of the term 'dependency'. He notes the varied causes of dependency: life cycle, dependency of crisis, disablement, personality traits, socially/culturally defined. The causes can be set against categories of need: orientation, activities of daily living, occupation, social integration, economics, emotional, environmental. He calls for more focus on 'dependency relationships'.

Gillian Dalley's paper rightly alerts us to different meanings: not relying on others, remaining assertive and so on. The combination of lack of precision as to the meaning of independence with the presumption that it must be valuable (whatever it means) leads to dangerous confusion. In policy terms I have been in several discussions where I have raised the consequence of driving forward those services which lead to people's independence: what of services for people who are becoming more dependent?

Indeed, what we are faced with under the guise of beneficent policy is a lack of thinking about goals and processes. Perhaps it is time to scrap the word.

This becomes even more the case when we test out the place of independence in whatever we would assert are the objectives of welfare policy. I take these to be to provide services, where appropriate, to support people to live as well or as fully as possible. Such an overarching objective needs to be spelt out or terms such as independence and autonomy become ends in themselves. Of course there has to be a debate as to what is the meaning of fulfilment, living well (or whatever phrase is chosen) and of the means to promote its achievement. To ignore such a search for the essence of what it is that we want services to achieve risks making these services mechanical and inappropriate.

A further dimension is that of external structures or systems: how far do poor transport, bad housing or unsafe environments limit individuals' capacity to participate (and coincidentally to be independent)?

I have suggested that living in a residential home too often is like living in someone else's home, in that people do not feel free to live as they would wish and have to account for themselves to others. Gillian Dalley puts the other side of this question: what is it about one's own home that we value? We could examine this further by looking at work undertaken on the meaning of home, but I think we should also try to search for what is important about the relationship of a person to the building in which they live, for in that relationship are found some of the core components of identity. That is not to say that it is the building, or the relationship to the building, that constructs identity. However, it is to assert that in some ways we test and support who we are by the construction of our lives in the places where we live.

I do not think that whatever it is that we prize as being important about 'own home' has to be found by ownership. Nor do I accept that simply telling residents that the ten square metres of personal space in a residential home is theirs to live in as they like is sufficient to establish what I want in the sense of 'own homeness'. Nor does 'own homeness' have to come from the home where one has been living. It can be established when we move house. It is imperative to search for the components of 'own homeness' so that consideration can be given to how these components can be found (or constructed) in a variety of housing settings and a variety of models of service provision. I would suggest that these include:

- involvement in decision making both about one's own life and the housing and service provision;

- considering the nature of the community of people living in the housing scheme and their relationship to the wider community; and

● sufficient personal space.

I have argued since 1981 that the living arrangements, whether in private home, housing with care, residential or nursing home should be seen as housing so that the same attitudes that pervade the provision of housing should become the norm within the different types of housing setting. People whether as tenants, part owners or owners should be able to participate in the place where they live, the services which they receive and the lives that they lead.

Many descriptors such as independence lose their subtlety (and indeed their life) as they become mechanised. All of us trade off one aspect for another, sometimes between competing positives, sometimes negatives. We settle for more of this and less of that. Terms like independence and autonomy are not absolutes, and must not become so in policy and service directives. That is the reason why I think words such as involvement capture better the dimensions of what have to be considered in housing and service provision. The points seem almost too obvious to need to be made: we move in and out of dependence throughout our lives; sometimes this leads to us managing tasks without the support of others for most of our lives; sometimes we need others to help us with certain tasks most of the time; sometimes we do tasks for ourselves and sometimes want (and sometimes need) others to do them for us; this can vary with our physical and our emotional state.

Demanding that policy objectives are focused on maintaining or promoting independence may lead to a lack of awareness of what people want in service provision, in which our own former experiences of being dependent may play a part. Indeed, Miller and Gwynne (1972), in examining a residential home for people with a physical disability noted the attractiveness of what they termed a horticultural model, in which people looked for growth and development. However, they saw the limitations of this and recognised the importance of organising for independence and organising for support.

Rather than driving without thought to an ill defined and confused concept of independence, we should try to understand more of what encourages people to live as fully as possible, doing things for themselves and valuing their lives, coupled with understanding of their lives in relation to others as friends and helpers. Without doing this, simplistic models are asserted in which it is presumed that the complexity of managing one's life is overcome by becoming a consumer, with money to buy services. Thankfully, life is more complex and resists such analysis.

References

Booth, T (1985) *Home Truths*, Aldershot: Gower.

Clough, R (1981) *Old Age Homes*, London: Allen and Unwin.

Miller, E and Gwynne, C (1972) *A Life Apart*, London: Tavistock.

Tizard, J *et al.* (1975) *Varieties of Residential Experience*, London: Routledge and Kegan Paul.

Wilkin, D (1989) *Users' Guide to Dependency Measures for Elderly People*, Sheffield: Joint Unit for Social Services Research, Sheffield University.

Willcocks, D, Peace, S and Kellaher, L (1987) *Private Lives in Public Places*, London: Tavistock.

3 Is genuine choice a reality?

The range and adequacy of living arrangements
available to older people

Leonie Kellaher

Introduction

This publication is about radical thinking and new responses to
aspects of later life to do with the day-to-day environments in
which people live as they grow older. I want to consider the
present, but also look into the future, with all the demographic
certainties and possibilities it may contain for older cohorts, as
they weigh up their living arrangements. What do older people
do in making such decisions, and what might they want to do?

Do older people: Plan? Hope for? Accept? Opt for? Drift into?
Put up with? Adapt to? Personalise? Or do they in fact **choose**?

I shall explore these issues through posing a number of questions. How important is it that there is available a wide range of
types of housing, in various kinds of locations, either connected
with particular co-residential living arrangements, or not, from
which people can select? Linked with this are questions of accessibility, affordability and eligibility; in other words with critical
pathways towards particular ends. Is either of these sets of factors
predominant? What do we mean, or intend to mean, by
'genuine' as applied to choice? In addressing these questions I
want to arrive not so much at a resolution, but at a way of
thinking and at a new disposition to act which is grounded in
what we know about what older people do in the crucial area of
living arrangements, and what we know about why they adopt
certain strategies.

Choice and the choosing implied is the privileged term

amongst the terms mentioned above. But I am going to argue that we need to appreciate older people's engagement in the less etherial, less ideal versions of decision making covered by most of these other terms. We might detect a sub-text in the title, which infers that any 'choices' made or attempted by older people are either imperfect or constrained by the inadequacy of what is on offer. That the pathways to choice may be obstructed or the contexts for choosing be fractured, so that good things on offer to others are presently, and perhaps structurally, beyond older people. It is more complex than this. I am not going to list or suggest new forms of housing and living arrangements, but since range and adequacy are important aspects of decision making, I am going to refer to some of the examples, old, new and speculative, of which we know something. I want to focus on what we know about the processes whereby older people make decisions which lead them in certain directions for their living arrangements.

What we have labelled 'choice' is an extremely complex phenomena, especially so when it comes to matters which concern identity construction and maintenance of self and in this, housing and the dwelling place are very important, if not central. Complexity is all the more apparent when the object of choice is such that it cannot readily be discarded if the 'fit' turns out to be a poor one, one that compromises the identity of the subject. This case has sometimes been made in respect of the difficulty in reversing choices to move into a residential or nursing home, not least because time and energy, emotional and physical, are in short supply for all concerned, particularly for the older person.

Rather than suggesting that this has to do with crude links between the supply and demand sides of a market, I am suggesting that decisions about where to live are made up of mixes of imagining, aspiration, wariness, hope, belief, caution, apprehension and calculation – all of which are more or less linked to ideas about self and others and, then, to more or less strategic and rational actions. Ideas about the nature of consumption may come into play since they draw upon notions of image and fit. However, for older people the 'target' to be met may be a more capricious and fluid one than for groups at younger ages; their circumstances are likely to change over just a few years, and they will need to re-imagine themselves in new settings. I am also saying that understanding how people manage such a complex constellation of feelings, responses and reactions, may not always be discursively accessible and that we need to examine very carefully what older people have actually *done* to arrive at certain living arrangements. What older people say or indicate may *not* have been possible is equally, if not more, important, as are any suggestions as to what may remain unconsidered, about the capacity of the material and social worlds which constitute living arrangements, to give individuals seeking to maintain self some room for manoeuvre.

If terms such as opt for, adapt, drift into, etc, as noted above, suggest levels of motivation and agency, the sub-headings appended to the title – own home, co-housing, retirement housing, sheltered housing, extra care housing, residential/ nursing homes and perhaps newer nomenclatures such as lifetime homes and universal design – infer three important dimensions of living arrangements.

Firstly, the materiality of a building in a particular setting, along with an internal spatial configuration and importantly, as I will show, its contents, both furniture which takes up floor space, as well as smaller objects;

Secondly, a social configuration or arrangement entailing self and others – kin or non-kin; friends or professionals;

Thirdly, help of various kinds and intensities.

These dimensions are very closely interconnected, however I shall lay particular emphasis throughout this paper on the first.

Realities, assumptions and possibilities

There are four things that must be addressed.

- An outline of the current pattern of older people's living arrangements.

- How far this measures up to what we know about how older people react to the living arrangements they have arrived at.

- An identification of the kinds of assumptions or premises the existing pattern is founded upon and sustained by.

- Whether all this might be re-cast for the future, and if so, how?

I am drawing upon material from several studies, but especially on the EPSRC EQUAL study with the title 'From Domesticity to Care', undertaken with Hanson and Rowlands at University

College, London (2001), which we hope will be made available by the Housing Corporation in 2002. This study has tried to explore the finer detail of older people's everyday lives in the context of home, with its many material and social facets. Using data from this study I hope to shed some light upon older people's thinking and actions in relation to changing or sticking with their current living arrangements. First though, I wish to set the wider scene by looking at what is known about where older people in this country live, and the kinds of dwellings they occupy in different kinds of locations and neighbourhoods as this enables a reading of the outcomes to so-called choices.

The current pattern of older people's living arrangements

Although it is familiar terrain, it seems important to acknowledge again the institutional–domestic distinction, since this has dominated policy and research for many decades and, I would also argue, has influenced all older people's strategic thinking about their living arrangements. Around 90 per cent of post-retired people live in the 'ordinary' domestic setting and end their days there – give or take a few days/weeks in a hospital/hospice or residential/nursing home setting at the very end of life. So 'ordinary' defines as 'extraordinary' the institutional settings in which around 5 per cent of the post-retired live out their days. This increases to a quarter when people – predominantly women – reach their eighties. These 'facts' and the need to re-cast them were challenged in the first paper by Gillian Dalley (chapter 2), and certainly need to be linked with this discussion. But for now, I will focus upon the majority, the 90 per cent, in their 'ordinary' domestic settings.

I will start with aspects of living arrangements which have to do with the building shell in its particular setting and the spatial patterning inside and beyond this shell associated with older people's lives. Several sets of distinctions are made in the policy and statistical literature. These frequently distinguish within 'ordinary' housing the mainstream and sheltered categories in which non-institutionally based older people live.

House type

Nine out of ten older people live in mainstream housing (90 per cent); the rest in sheltered housing (10 per cent). The English

House Condition Survey (EHCS) (DETR 1996) identifies eight types and seven periods and aggregates these two categories. Table 3.1 shows all building periods against house type for the population as a whole.

Table 3.1 English House Condition Survey, 1996

	Pre-1850	1850–99	1900–18	1919–44	1945–64	1965–80	1980–>	All%
Purpose-built, hi-rise flat	*	*	*	*	0.6	0.8	*	1.6
Purpose-built, lo-rise flat	*	*	0.4	1.2	3.4	4.8	3.1	13.2•
Converted flat	0.3	2.5	1.2	0.2	*	0.2	*	4.5
Bungalow	*	0.1	0.1	1.3	2.8	4.0	1.8	10.2•
Detached house	1.5	0.8	0.5	2.2	2.2	4.3	4.0	15.4•
Semi-detached house	0.7	1.4	1.4	8.9	7.9	4.3	1.7	26.3
Medium-large terraced	0.7	3.4	2.8	2.5	2.4	3.2	0.7	15.7
Small terraced	0.4	2.9	1.9	2.7	1.5	1.6	2.0	13.1
All	3.7	11.4	8.4	19.1	21.0	23.2	13.2	100

*Denotes too few in the category to register

If we consider this matrix showing the types of housing occupied by the population generally, and then look at the concentrations of house types in which older people are most likely to live (*marked* •), we see that some cells are not characterised by concentrations of older people's housing types – high-rise flats for instance. Others, notably bungalows and, though the numbers are small, detached houses are much more likely to be older people's territories, irrespective of whether they own or rent.

The pattern is complicated and may be changing, for example, the adaptation of tower blocks (e.g. Glasgow, Hackney) for older people. One in ten of older people, in increasing proportions with advancing years (4 per cent at 65 years compared with 20 per cent at 85 years +), lives in what is labelled sheltered housing, which may mean there is a warden, that services are available (personal, care and/or domestic help). Purpose built low-rise flats and bungalows are likely to characterise sheltered housing, across different tenures.

Which brings us to patterns of tenure. We know that an increasing proportion of the post-retired population is in owner occupation, presently around two thirds of elderly households are owner occupiers. Not surprisingly, it is the younger post-retired who are most likely to own, though one in ten of the over seventy-fives is also an owner. Nearly two thirds (61 per cent) of these own outright (ONS 2000). A quarter of older households are social housing renters, most likely to be in purpose-built flats, with a tendency at advancing years to move towards residential social landlords (RSLs) and away from local authorities, though on the whole, RSL tenants tend to be slightly younger than council tenants. Five per cent of renters are in the private sector. These people are more likely to include the oldest than those just entering retirement and to be split between the residual category renting from landlords in converted flats and those who rent in the newer private sector.

Location

The geographical place in which older people live is undoubtedly important for identity construction. However, whilst policy makers may explain this importance in terms of familiarity – of places and people – I would suggest that this familiarity takes a particular form. It has to do with the being part of a social network of some kind and this is what influences decisions as to where to live in later years. Geographical proximity to the people who are significant links in the network is likely to be important but not necessarily so; other calculations enter into this and proximity may be overridden. What seems to be important is that one can play a part, however small and however peripherally, in a network that provides at least the possibility of contact and help at a number of levels and intensities. This may, on occasions, entail decisions to be at a distance.

The categories through which the distribution of the older population across the country can be described are familiar enough. Region is at the macro end of the continuum with neighbourhood at the other. Then there are the categories such as – metropolitan, urban, suburban, rural – coastal, etc, which describe the settings. The ACORN classification system (a sampling system for socio-economic groupings) uses census data to identify location categories derived from socio-cultural features; several of these include factors to do with age, and old age. For example, there are 'rural areas of affluent greys', 'retirement areas of prosperous pensioners', 'mature home-owning areas' and 'council estate, low income areas – older people – less prosperous'. This is just one way of describing neighbourhoods where older people live, but again there can be a layered and multidimensional picture or one that simply looks at the broad outlines. Where neighbourhood is concerned, categories are more likely to be constructed by taking account of factors that are more or less socially generated. Thus, they may be thought of as declining/ageing, regenerating, static, and new development. Connectedness with local facilities may also be brought into play.

Some regions are characterised by concentrations of older people, coastal towns for example and rural concentrations, such as the South West. This clustering is partly a consequence of post-retirement migratory decisions, though also a residue of out-migration by younger groups in search of work, often to metropolitan and urban areas. Certain neighbourhoods, Clerkenwell in East London for instance, are no longer spoken of as declining inner city neighbourhoods, with residual populations of poor older people; regeneration has taken over and replaced, if not displaced, these older generations. At the same time, other small areas have relatively invisible concentrations of older people, sometimes attached to incoming minority ethnic groups, as well as those who have aged in place.

This patterning of housing type and location in relation to older people's dwelling places is clearly shaped by many influences. We may be able to explain the patterns fairly satisfactorily in terms of demographics and economics. But how are we to understand these kinds of distributions in terms of choice and older people? What kinds of decisions, within what contexts of constraint and opportunity, have been made by these older householders as to where to live and what kind of house to occupy? Just taking the distributions found within EHCS for instance one may conclude that older people are constrained or barred from occupying each and every type of housing; that they choose not to; that they are not regarded – or do not see themselves – as eligible or suitable for each and every category; or that history and cohort factors, along with cultural preferences, are at work. The same question applies to tenure and region or neighbourhood: how far are these a consequence of decisions? The point of raising these details which concern the location and character of the dwelling 'shell', and there are many more factors which could be drawn in, is to illustrate the range of macro-scale factors which have a bearing on, or frame, living arrangements. It is also to lay the ground for the part of my argument that concerns what older people can actually do about where they decide to live. Before addressing this, however, I want to say something about the internal spatial configurations that characterise older people's living arrangements. Whereas, house type and location are not readily or immediately amenable to adaptation, other interior aspects of living arrangements may be more so.

Internal arrangements

It is arguable that the amount of space available within a dwelling is an over-arching factor when choosing accommodation. Taking all ages, in all dwellings the EHCS shows that nationally, the average floor space, per person, is 43m^2, for lone person households this rises to 66m^2. Older owner occupiers have even more floor space than those in younger age groups, with 78m^2. This means, that in nearly three million households, generally in suburban or rural locations, there are people on their own or as a couple, in homes with three or more bedrooms and a good deal of space. However, there remain another four million older households with less than this amount of space in which to arrange their lives. Some of these are also owner occupiers with slightly more restricted spatial arrangements, often in more recently purpose-built flats. Others live in accommodation provided by local authorities and RSLs, also purpose-built. We should not cast adrift the statistically small proportion of older people, but significant numerically, who live in residential and nursing home settings.

Those who rent, across tenures and at all ages, have slightly less space than have owner occupiers. Whether this is less space than they want is partly illuminated through the General Household Survey (ONS 2000) report. The great majority of older households (80 per cent) were reported as 'above bedroom standard' which is to say they had at least one bedroom more than the minimum standard. The term 'under-occupied' may be applied to such households. In the population as a whole, 70 per cent of households were 'above bedroom standard'. At the same time, only 18 per cent of household informants considered that they had too much space; older persons households were twice as likely as younger ones to say this, though numbers are still small. The group most likely to say they had too few bedrooms was the group who were RSL tenants. Only 10 per cent, however, voiced dissatisfaction with the size of rooms, a small proportion that gets even smaller with age. There are clearly issues here that have to do with the connection of standards to the lives that are lived on the ground.

Analysis from the EPSRC study, 'From Domesticity to Care', shows that the more 'special' the provision, those that the oldest old are likely to gravitate, particularly as RSL tenants, the less space is available, generally in terms of a second bedroom. A detailed analysis of spatial features also shows that such 'special' dwellings are likely to have gradations between what we understand as public and private spaces which are either very compressed or less complex in spatial terms. There are other important points to be flagged up in relation to internal arrangements. The condition of the property is clearly crucial and must play a part in decision making. A significant minority (14 per cent) of older households do not have central heating, the oldest old are most likely to be so deprived. Dissatisfaction with the state of repair was much higher amongst tenants (social and private combined) than with owner occupiers (23 per cent cf. 8 per cent). Similar differentials emerged when it came to the appearance of the dwelling: 26 per cent of tenants compared with 6 per cent of owner occupiers reported dissatisfaction with the way their house looked. Features that have a bearing on feelings of security, such as whether the dwelling is at ground-floor level or higher seems to be associated with being in a couple or alone, illustrating the close links between the social and material aspects of living arrangements.

Social configurations and living arrangements

Couple households are the most common at ages under 75, and the increase observed over the last two decades is projected to continue and include even older groups. Living alone is still most likely for those over 75, though this has increased for all older people (by 30 per cent since the 1980s), a consequence of divorce as well as of death rates. Those living in miscellaneous households (often siblings, parent and adult child) have decreased by nearly 40 per cent over the last two decades, and now account for only one in ten of older households. These social arrangements are closely linked to the housing factors outlined above. Those living alone are most likely to be in some form of sheltered housing, only 5 per cent of couples and 2 per cent of other 'pairs' are in such settings compared to 17 per cent of people living alone. This form of housing is associated with advanced years (4 per cent of 65-69 year olds compared to 20 per cent of those aged 85 years and older, live in sheltered settings).

It is now less the norm for household groupings to consist of kin, that is to say, of people linked through ties of blood or marriage. Cohabitation – of heterosexual and homosexual couples – has altered the statistical picture of households. The projection of increased numbers of older couple households is just starting to take account of this, as is the case where ageing families of ethnic minorities are concerned. The point to be made, however, within the context of this paper is that the older households of the future are likely to be similar in size – lone person or duos – and to be linked affectively, though perhaps not juridically. At the same time, there may well be more fluid arrangements, with movements – long or short term – across and between households. There are also incipient indications that linkings of more than two individuals may emerge, for example, where economic considerations take precedence over affective factors, co-ownership is one instance of this. The social configurations which now characterise households, and which may come to do so in the future, are integral to the kinds of informal support systems which develop and upon which formal systems depend.

Help of various kinds and intensities

Households have always been economic units whether or not they were founded on strong emotional ties. Many anthropologists have argued that mutual support through economic benefit – entailing bringing up the next generation – is the basis of any kinship system and its accompanying domestic arrangements (Sahlins 1976). The pattern in England has been to take help for granted, within and between kin groups and, to a lesser extent, between friendship/neighbour/acquaintance groups. Testimony to this is that where very elderly spouses survive, the less frail is expected (and expects) to help the more frail partner. Most commonly the spouse helps in cases of need, followed by other household members and then by non-household relatives. When the need for help – which may come to be called 'care' – becomes intense, the costs often exceed the resources of the domestic unit and external forces have to be called up. The level of such costs is increasing whilst the external reserves from which care is drawn are in decline.

A distinction might be made between domestic and personal help and care, but it is arguable that it is the volume and intensity of the help needed from outside the household or family unit – whether it is personal or domestic – which is critical. The need to arrange help, often intensive, and to finance it on a continuous basis often triggers more deliberate decisions about living arrangements than may previously have been the case in people's lives.

Having given an overview of the patterning of older people's actual living arrangements I now want to examine the links with decision making and perhaps choice, on the part of older people. Firstly, it seems undeniable that there is a considerable range of complex possibilities here. Whether complexity equates with adequacy and range is another question. Adequacy, in terms of quantity of space and condition, appears to be such that expressed dissatisfaction levels are low. Yet we cannot afford to be sanguine about this

I now wish to look at how far this set of present patterns measure up with what we know about the actuality of how older people arrive at their choices around living arrangements

Reaction of older people to their living arrangements

I am again drawing upon the EPSRC EQUAL study, 'From Domesticity to Care' to illustrate what people do at home to improve the 'fit' of the domestic setting. We have very detailed data, from sixty older people and their homes, to consider against a backdrop of 240 dwellings for which we just have floor plans and not the older person's commentary on the ways adaptations have occurred. This larger sample, however, is mostly housing for older people – which includes sheltered units. For comparison, we have added some plans for single rooms (e.g. student accommodation, young single people's and prisoners' rooms/cells), so the data set runs from mainstream housing through to age-specific, highly-serviced, communal accommodation. Using this sample at the two levels of detail we can consider older people's homes from three points of view:

- space standards and self-containment;
- internal layout and plan configuration;
- space use for domestic activities.

We have proposed a continuum from domesticity to institutional living, which relates to:

- the amount and scale of the space under the occupant's direct control;
- the extent to which the layout/configuration of the dwelling reflects both personal need and preferences as well as widely accepted conventions for organising domestic space;
- the embedding in the dwelling of a well defined privacy gradient.

Space standards

Table 3.2 uses thirty-two groupings of accommodation type, parallel with those used by the EHCS, and shows the following spatial arrangements: trends for total space across different dwelling forms constructed over the last century to date; its allocation across areas designated for daily living activities.

Very broadly, the points to make are that space declines with more recent designs; and that the sharpest decrease in allocation is to be found in purpose-built housing for older people in the social renting sector. It may be that more economical – and ergonomic – use is being made of less space. Having said this, there are examples of housing for special groups, such as those requiring extra care and having dementia, where more space has been allowed. Interestingly, in the private sector space in bungalows and retirement flats is a third greater than for corresponding types in the social rented sector.

Internal layout and plan configuration

The dwellings in which our detailed sample of sixty older people live are generally more spatially generous than in the larger, comparative sample. However, there are some trends of interest.

Table 3.2 From domesticity to care? Overall space and allocation for daily living (square metres) across a range of dwelling types

MAINSTREAM	Floor areas	Habitable	Cooking	Bathing	Circulation	Storage
Post-war terraced	75.24	48.85	9.34	4.39	8.46	4.20
Contemporary terraced	58.62	37.55	5.53	5.49	7.63	2.42
*Terraced	**82.20**	**51.38**	**9.50**	**4.89**	**12.52**	**3.91**
Post-war semi-det	68.18	44.87	8.76	4.52	8.47	2.24
Contemp. semi-det	67.22	44.26	6.49	5.70	8.56	2.23
*Semi-detached	**101.19**	**67.51**	**12.16**	**4.11**	**12.48**	**2.53**
Post-war detached	87.72	58.47	8.51	6.28	11.79	2.77
Contemp. detached	94.20	58.78	12.01	8.58	11.52	3.31
Lifetime homes	84.38	51.66	10.01	7.62	12.00	3.08
Post-war bungalows	61.22	38.51	8.19	4.70	7.02	1.80
Sheltered bungalows	46.68	29.64	6.59	3.81	4.23	2.41
*Bungalows – private	**74.22**	**44.82**	**10.83**	**4.24**	**6.13**	**6.40**
*Bungalows – sheltered	**38.86**	**23.02**	**7.59**	**3.30**	**3.86**	**1.10**
Post-war lo-rise flats	60.96	37.95	8.01	5.19	6.99	2.82
Contemp. lo-rise flats	72.71	46.81	8.08	6.82	8.91	2.02
*Purp-built lo-rise flats	**50.51**	**34.32**	**5.89**	**3.44**	**5.76**	**1.11**
Sheltered flats 1945/64	47.15	30.21	6.69	3.81	4.4	2.03
Sheltered flats 1965/80	39.25	25.23	5.12	3.19	3.21	2.51
Sh. flats–cont. La/RSL	39.15	26.98	5.84	3.79	5.00	1.18
Private retire flats/cont.	61.40	39.27	6.82	5.31	7.45	2.56
Extra-care frail eld. flts	44.30	28.72	5.59	4.71	3.90	1.33
*Sheltered flats- CI	**48.06**	**30.14**	**6.63**	**3.83**	**4.90**	**3.24**
*Sheltered flats CIIa	**35.60**	**21.99**	**5.07**	**3.47**	**3.62**	**3.24**
*Sheltered flats CIIb	**40.83**	**25.95**	**5.54**	**3.28**	**4.32**	**1.73**

Table 3.2 *(continued)*

MAINSTREAM	Floor areas	Habitable	Cooking	Bathing	Circulation	Storage
Mobility/lifetime flats	50.98	34.84	5.67	4.44	4.78	1.46
*Converted flats	**72.13**	**43.19**	**10.22**	**5.73**	**9.91**	**3.08**
Nursing home rooms	14.81	13.06	——	1.29	.40	.06
Residential home room	11.97	11.03	——	.60	.12	.21
*Nurs/resid homes	**16.61**	**15.18**	——	**1.42**	**0000**	**0000**
Dementia unit rooms	18.76	12.96	——	3.48	2.02	.29
Young people's rooms	18.32	13.02	1.61	1.90	1.15	.64
Single people's rooms	19.86	16.00	——	2.58	.73	.55

The categories in **bold** and with * are from the detailed data on sixty older people; the others are the sample of floor plans

Cooking space exceeds that given to the bathroom/wc in all instances except the institutional settings where cooking space has generally been eliminated. The balance between these two service spaces is, however, rather variable, the more recent the building the less the differential between the two. Service space is most limited in the sheltered flats, whether recent or older. This is accompanied by a reduction in differential cooking/bathing spaces. Cooking space ranges between taking up three quarters of the available service space in older mainstream housing to just over half in more recent buildings. It would seem that spatial allocations for older people (except for lifetime homes and mobility/lifetime flats, where more bathing space has been allowed) appears to have translated into cooking and bathing space at bare minimum levels. Nonetheless, it would also appear that all the conventional spaces – those deemed necessary for a decent, ordinary life – are present, however minimally.

In terms of the way this space is arranged, when we look at the number of separate spaces associated with each type of dwelling and the associated distribution of overall floor space, we find a sharp decline from the highly differentiated spaces typical of older mainstream housing to just three or four separate spaces in sheltered housing and one or sometimes two in settings which can be described as communities or institutions.

This has implications for what has been called the 'privacy gradient' (Robinson *et al.* 1996). This is based on two linked hypotheses: first, that spaces in single family homes are usually arranged in terms of depth from the main threshold to reflect a hierarchy from most public to most private areas; second, Robinson proposed three distinct patterns of connection between spaces: linear sequences with circulation areas; radiating patterns off a central entrance hall; and triangular arrangements connecting public, habitable spaces. The argument goes further to suggest that each pattern is associated with different kinds of access and control over domestic space. Evans (1997) supports this to a certain extent, proposing that interconnectivity reflects sociability – a more public mode perhaps, and the linear arrangement is more conducive to the control of privacy. Robinson makes the point that institutional buildings are not characterised by very subtle gradations along the privacy gradient. This is something to which I will return, but next I want to comment on how the sixty older informants, whose houses were measured up precisely and with whom we had lengthy interviews, said they made their homes work for them. This group covered a good age range and had diverse levels of capacity and frailty. Some had a lot of contact with family and friends, others had only very thin networks of tenuous connections. Most lived on their own. All were making a go of living at home; none had given up, most – even the very frail – took great pride in their homes and were actively engaged in home improvements, decoration and internal re-arrangements.

Space use for domestic activities

The kinds of spaces we are talking about have been outlined above. What do older people think about these and how do spatial configurations fit alongside daily living and the maintenance of self that I proposed at the outset as being a central goal for all older people in their homes? I have already mentioned the low levels of dissatisfaction reported for older people generally with their housing; something that declines even further with age. Our sixty informants were similarly silent as to dissatisfactions. How is this to be interpreted? One comment in the General Household Survey (ONS 2000) suggested that owner occupiers might be less likely to express dissatisfaction with the appearance of their homes than tenants, because criticism would reflect back on them. Dissatisfaction may then be associated with reduced levels of control. It would be true to the EPSRC data overall to interpret silence on this matter, not merely as an absence of problems or dissatisfaction, but as contentment, even pleasure, at having circumvented design deficits and manoeuvred within spatial constraints. One informant said:

> *With being in this room quite often, I think to myself: I can't move anything there because of the radiator. I can't have a lot of furniture, but that settee was over here last week and my TV was there and this chair was near the window. Oh yes, I make sure that everything gets moved around.*

Another explained:

> *I do change the furniture around and I think it is a bit of a tonic.*

Bedroom space

Many informants had down-sized their bedroom furniture to fit bedrooms smaller than those they had come from. For some this had been a wrench, but even they invariably became reconciled by weighing up the gains they perceived in terms of convenience and security. Some people had taken the opportunity to start afresh with new things to match their new setting.

Apart from those in residential/nursing home settings (3), all had separate sleeping spaces. A number had created secondary sleeping places in the sitting or dining rooms for guests. The need for a 'spare' room was almost universal and is in line with the pattern reported above from the General Household Survey on 'under-occupation'. Where people did not want or have a spare room for guests, they described the need or use of such a space for interests and, in the case of several of the younger old, for an office to house a computer and electronic equipment.

> *Every home is going to need a small, sort-of office. A computer is not like a television, where it can be part of the furniture; it's a working thing. I've kept it up there [in the converted, spare bedroom] and called it an office ... because it's got to be an entirely separate thing.*

The guest rooms provided for tenants' visitors in sheltered

housing did not always fit the bill because the need to make a reservation ruled out more spontaneous dropping in of family; grandchildren were mentioned specifically. Finally, a few informants valued their second bedroom for a live-in carer, in one case an alcove had been partitioned off from the living room.

Dining-kitchen spaces

On average, kitchen space in the detailed sample was 7.67m². Whilst the design guidance is not clear on what size a kitchen should be, it is not really possible to use the kitchen for eating at a table if it is much less than 12m². Most people managed with what they had; many informants said that they varied the place where they took their meals: sometimes in front of the TV, sometimes on what was usually a drop-leaf table in the main living space. This variation appeared to be important as one way of ordering the daytime, as well as a strategy to ameliorate the impact of having to eat alone.

> *The most solitary occupation there is, is having a meal on your own … I don't like it so I have a tray in here and I read, or watch TV or just think.*

> *I continue to have meals at a table, like I did with my husband. That's what I think you should do. It makes life more like a home, like a family.*

Bathroom space

The average size of the bathrooms/wcs in our detailed sample is 3.81m², thus approaching the average for the UK as a whole (3.87m²). The size for a wheelchair accessible bathroom is 5.1m². The reduced space of bathrooms has implications for managing at home, though again, nearly all informants managed some kind of arrangement. Getting in and out of the bath was, however, often ruled out as too hazardous.

Living rooms

There is much more detail to report on how these older people arranged their daily lives, frequently in somewhat restricted spaces. There are two points I wish to make which will lead us on to some reflections then to tentative conclusions. First, the numbers of items of furniture people had in their living rooms. We took detailed inventories of everything that took up floor space and found that there were universally double those which illustrate guidance for design. This was true whether people had just moved in or were long established and across gender. The inference here, and this might be directed at policy makers and others involved with determining standards, is that older people's material worlds are much more complex than outsiders might generally be prepared to grant.

This complexity is reflected in the multiple activity areas older people set up in their living rooms. Regardless of space allowances, areas had generally been marked out for sitting, guests places often distinguished from the home owner's chair; for dining; for watching television and for interests/hobbies – sewing, genealogy and woodwork are just three examples. Such sub-spaces were defined by the strategic arrangement of furniture. Where there was a bed in the living space, the orientation of the room, through the positioning of furniture, was such that the visitor did not have to view this 'inappropriate' sub-space head on. In the small number of instances where informants had large houses they allocated a room to each of these activities.

Similarly, a buffer space was often set up at the entrance to the living room where this was off an internal circulation space, as in some sheltered housing schemes. The point I wish to make here, and I could give many more examples of the strategic creativity of our informants in re-shaping the space of their homes, is that they invariably required something more from the building than it initially offered. Moreover, that without any expressions of serious dissatisfaction, these older people set about engineering more satisfactory arrangements for themselves and others who came to see them at home.

In many cases, as shown by the spatial data I have already outlined, older people may face quite formidable challenges. That they tackle these and achieve solutions that clearly satisfy them is testimony to two things. Firstly, that they have a strong sense of what is proper in the domestic setting, particularly which spatial configurations are appropriate for them personally and culturally. Secondly, that finding the right fit between dwelling and the self is extremely important. Some of our informants were very frail and not capable of moving things, even with help. Nonetheless, they achieved this through social networks and systems of debt and obligation they set up with family – real and fictive – and sometimes others. The thing that seems to be important is to present the self, both to oneself and to others, as a complex, multidimensional entity. This becomes very difficult in the uni-cellular space of the bedsitter or residential room, which cannot easily reveal multiple aspects of personality and experience.

The assumptions that sustain existing patterns and the premises upon which they are founded

The data I have offered here indicates, first of all, an inclination on the part of society, manifest in the guidance from designers, endorsed through policy and embedded in practice, to place older people in smaller spaces than those occupied by other age groups. This is not a new observation: Townsend's theory of structured dependency might be invoked in support of it (Townsend 1981); Foucault's propositions around societal constraints can be accommodated (Foucault 1977). Powell Lawton's theory of environmental press might also lend itself to supporting down-sizing, since many older people aim for domestic settings which will remain manageable as physical capacities become uncertain, though it is fair to say that Powell Lawton wrote with release from repression in view. Neither is it new to remark on the silence, if not acquiescence, of older people concerning their living arrangements (Lawton 1980).

I think it is new, however, to show that older people resist these restrictive spatial impositions wherever possible, though without fanfare. They hang on to that extra space, they build in complexity where it has been 'written out' because they need to do so to give expression to the complexity of selves that have experience over seven, eight or nine decades. People attempt, and frequently succeed, in re-configuring their space to be more appropriate – to be a better fit, not just with the past and the present, but in anticipation of a future that may hold unknown incapacities and adjustments. Older people recognise that even where individuals and couples do not live within close kinship contexts, domestic space still needs to reflect the relationships between inhabitants and visitors (most older people receive guests weekly if not daily (ONS 2000)). This may entail more complex morphology than many providers are accustomed to make available in purpose-built housing for older people.

The tendency to plan within low space standards for older

people would seem to arise from an assumption that ageing entails a reduction in domestic activities and also in people's social networks and encounters in and beyond the home. It is arguable that this has led to balances between the private and more public aspects of home life in favour of a more scaled down – ostensibly intimate – world. The reduction, if not elimination, of a privacy gradient in some housing sectors, to a small world centred on the living room, suggests a view that older people do not inhabit the wider world. Whilst such assumptions are likely to impinge on all older people, it is those who live as tenants who tend to face the greatest challenges – sometimes endorsed through local authority policies intended to 'un-block' family dwellings. One only has to look at *Saga Magazine* to see later years promoted as a time of expansiveness and opportunity. But we must also acknowledge that this is only now being built into living arrangements with the suggestion that lifestyle opportunities can replace worries about maintaining property, security and getting help as and when needed, though almost exclusively in the private sector.

Policies relating to eligibility and access to a scarce resource such as sheltered housing are obviously implicated. However, as just noted, we also see older owner occupiers moving to tenancies or taking leases in the private or not-for-profit sectors, with a sense of relief that some of the unpredictabilities associated with ageing may have been forestalled. Whilst it may be true that many, if not all older people see a move to more convenient, sometimes smaller, arrangements as desirable, I think the evidence points to there being limits below which spatial allocations and configurations should not fall if culturally decent – inclusive – lives are to be conducted.

'Young-old' owner occupiers would appear to be in advantageous positions, having resources to exploit freedom and opportunity. There is little indication that this group finds the range or adequacy of provision wearisome or limiting, especially since everyone improvises, invents and manoeuvres at home, not just out of necessity but also creatively and as a way of attaching to the place they live in. What of the other groups? Those approaching or beyond 85 or so, no longer with a supportive partner, with mobility limitations occasioned by unpredictable health and strength, or levels of confidence previously taken for granted now eroded? As owner occupiers, we know from Askham's research (Askham *et al.* 1999) that their houses may become problematic. This group has some scope to purchase housing with care and this market is expanding, though we still do not know if it can sustain sizeable numbers of older people, and there remains the problem of engaging suffi-cient skilled care personnel. Importantly, there seems to be some tacit equation involved which entails trading space, with all the messages it carries in terms of maintained identity, for help. In fact, this is often a transfer of resources from the tasks of constructing identity as a complex, capable person to one which requires 'support'. That this might be accompanied by reduced spatial arrangements in more 'special' settings, may well limit the kind of manoeuvres necessary to maintain self. Nonetheless, older people continue to resist spatial constraints even when they become very frail and occupy very limited spaces.

For the large minority which does not have property assets to convert into some degree of selection as to where to live and how to get help when needed, we might expect the problems to be compounded. The data from the EPSRC EQUAL study referred to earlier suggests that once in local authority or RSL sheltered housing, older people pick up the threads of home-making and work at trying to make the place fit them and their unpredictable mobility and health needs. They did not speak of greater limita-tions in ways which were markedly different from those who owned their houses. The furnishings, objects and ornaments in their living rooms, for instance, did not strike one as remarkably different to those of owner occupiers, and yet the range of housing options available to tenants who need something different as they grow older might be more restricted in certain ways.

Perhaps it is fair to argue that the difference between those who purchase and those who apply to rent is not so much what is on offer but the ability to reject options. Owner occupiers enjoy as much freedom to view the field, to decide which will be their field, and to reject options, as agents and providers will tolerate. Those who apply to rent in the public/RSL sector must demonstrate eligibility for what is a scarce resource. They reject offers – not options – at some risk. Neither group, however, are likely to make reference to a range – real or hypothetical – of options or offers from which the selection might have been made. At most, they are likely to describe the final selection between no more than two possibilities. Because many hidden factors are entailed in deciding and selecting, the options must be reduced so that all factors material, locational and social, can remain in play as the person imagines themselves, their connections, their preferences and the future possibilities, in a particular setting. To say that choice is 'genuine' when it is about confronting a full array of options renders a confusing disservice to older people. I would say, then, that something approaching choice may be achieved where it is possible to sift through several possibilities, discarding some and working others up into realities through imaginative calculation, something the tenant may not be able to do to the same extent as an owner occupier.

How might all this be re-cast for the future?

In considering their houses and homes, particularly when thinking around the idea of moving, older people are conservative. Overshadowed by the possibility that decisions may be taken out of their hands in an emergency, for instance, many consider taking evasive action before the point of crisis is reached. Sometimes this may mean leaving a dwelling prematurely rather than 'hoping' to die 'in place'. The aim of their moving or staying strategies is maintenance of self as a social being, central if possible, attached at least, to a network of family/friends/acquaintances. The house, its location, internal arrangements and presentation through day-to-day management, is the principle vehicle through which this is accomplished. In this sense the building and the material form of home is secondary, whilst being integral to identity.

I take this position, however, to argue that, firstly, the range of provision we have currently is quite broad and, secondly, older people are rather good at selecting something that they can work on to fulfil the goal of maintaining their social selves. This may be an edited version of the self at younger ages or it may be a re-envisaged self with incapacities in place, but our data shows how it is people's own ingenuity, even in difficult surroundings. What is required for older people to experience a sense of choice, rather than 'putting up with' and 'making do' is an appreciation – by those who plan and provide – of older people's motives on the home front and the mechanisms which structure their thinking and strategies. We do not necessarily need new forms of housing. What may be required is a simple system which indicates for each and every dwelling whether or not it can accommodate one of three levels of help. These might range from occasional help, personally or domestically through to intensive, skilled help because of infirmity or severely reduced mobility. New approaches to selection processes in the local authority/RSL sectors are also required to permit a sifting through several possibilities in a way which engenders a greater sense of control. Finally, any remnants of notions that supply and demand of housing for older people are crudely linked needs to be dispelled.

This is not to say that older people's options for later life living arrangements should be reduced or in any way circumscribed. But it is to say that no amount of prescription, description and invention of new or existing forms will enhance choice unless the pathways to decision making are better understood so that 'demand' can be registered as such and shaped into supply. Having said this, I have also been arguing that older people themselves will engineer the 'supply' end as they make their homes fit their lives and their selves.

Few professionals are likely to accept that it is as crude or simple as represented here, which is to say, an array of commodities is laid before the 'consumer' who, in possession of information and know-how, makes a selection determined by financial-economic considerations. The 'market' for housing, however, and I am including the social housing sector as part of the market, appears to be predicated on the assumption that the three elements are always directly linked. We need to understand more about patterns of consumption, especially the imaginings whereby people judge if a commodity – and sometimes housing is that – is the right 'fit'. Desire and interest need to be generated and I have put the case that selection rests on discarding many possibilities. The lifestyles being advertised for private sector housing is designed to suggest the probability of good fit between housing, aspirations and self. Importantly, in this relatively new sector, spatial standards appear to be quite generous and cultural conventions, as to what are decent and proper configurations generally observed, including sensitive privacy gradients.

Finally, with reference to the economic theory – that much is uncertain – proposed by Thorstein Veblen (1999), and now being employed in explanations for consumer interest, what is required it seems to me, is not CHOICE writ large, but some elbow room to see, discard and work upon.

References

Askham, J, Nelson, H, Tinker, A and Hancock, R (1999) *To Have and to Hold: the bond between older people and the homes they own*, York: York Publishing Service.

DETR (1998) *English House Condition Survey 1996*, London: The Stationery Office.

EPSRC EQUAL (2001) Hanson, J, Kellaher, L and Rowlands, M *Profiling the Housing Stock for Older People: the transition from domesticity to care*. Final report of EPSRC EQUAL Research, University College London.

Evans, R (1997) *Figures, doors and passages in translations from drawing to building and other essays*, London: AA Publishing.

Foucault, M (1977) *Discipline and Punish: the birth of the prison*, trans. Alan Sherridan, London: Allen Lane.

Lawton, MP (1980) E*nvironment and Ageing*, Monterey CA: Brooks/Cole.

ONS (2000) *Living in Britain: results from the 1998 general household survey*, London: The Stationery Office.

Robinson, J, Thompson, T, Deitreich, M, Ferris, M and Sinclair, V (1996) Architectural features and perceptions of community residences for people with mental retardation, *American Journal of Mental Retardation* 101(3): 292–313.

Sahlins, M (1979) *Stone Age Economics*, London: Tavistock Press.

Townsend, P (1980) The structured dependency of the elderly; the creation of social policy in the twentieth century, *Ageing and Society* 1(1): 65–28.

Veblen, T (1999) *International Journal of Politics, Culture and Society* 13(2) (Winter) special issue on T Veblen.

COMMENTARY 1

Sheila Peace

Leonie Kellaher's paper has presented us with some very innovative data from the EPSRC EQUAL study 'From Domesticity to Care'. This is material that will offer new ideas. In particular, the coming together of researchers from the disciplines of architecture and anthropology is important both for methodological development in terms of research and visibility in terms of the dissemination of information. It is not often that we get to examine the materiality of buildings alongside everyday experiences of people within one piece of research.

In considering my response it is therefore not surprising that I am drawn to the debate around 'motivation and agency' in late life with regard to where people are living. I think these terms are more useful than the word 'choice' over living environments which seems too clear cut and clinical, demanding of selection. For most of us real life is more complex and in some ways constrained, and from my experience of talking with older people about where they live, variations on the following scenario emerge. They may be seeking:

> The Right 'Space' in The 'Right' Place (sometimes if they have the 'right' face)
> but may end up in:
> The Right 'Space' in The 'Wrong' Place (material plus, social minus)
> Or
> The 'Wrong' Space in The 'Right' Place (material minus, social plus)

These three sentences encompass the areas that Leonie discusses in her paper concerning: materiality; social arrangements; and the range and intensity of help. I will outline briefly each of these areas in a moment. But first, I feel that the words 'motivation' and 'agency' bring us immediately to the world of the individual and I am conscious of the juxtaposition of individual and society or broader social factors. So I need to start at the collective level and recognise the constraints that may be set on individuality.

At this level I want to consider four overarching characteristics that can impact upon motivation and agency in relation to living arrangements: age itself; gender; culture, and income (see diagram on next page). These broader issues become guides for understanding individual behaviour. Each of these characteristics raises issues and also relate to each other. For example:

(a) *Age* – in defining later life we may be spanning a forty-year period. We can look at age in at least two ways. First, historically across the life course of the individual – so time is important and, second, at one point in time across a range of people of different ages. Both perspectives can affect choice of living arrangements. For example, the person in their eighties will have been born in the 1920s; the person in their sixties during the 1940s. If we look at parts of their *life course*: how will housing and social policy have affected them? Certain types of accommodation and forms of tenure have been more or less common in different time periods. Did people raise their families in the war years or the more affluent

	Age	Gender	Culture	Income
Housing History				
Under/ Over Occupation		CHOICE		
Privacy				
The Body		MOTIVATION	AGENCY	
Permeability Between External World Space Internal Living Space				

1960s? Did they make moves in terms of location for employment, for marriage or for retirement? These experiences will have affected their living arrangements at that time and will have led them to make certain decisions that may affect them now.

(b) *Gender* – we know that over the life course women utilise space within the home in different ways to men, e.g. they may have been more concerned over their children's need for privacy at different times of their lives rather than their own, or for having space for home-working (e.g. Matrix 1984, the work of Women's Design Service). Also in terms of ageing, we know that women live longer than men – even if that gap is closing. This difference in life expectancy means that more women will end their lives living alone. Yet roles within the family may influence living arrangements, e.g. the British Social Attitudes Survey (1999) found that 60 per cent of grandparents lived thirty minutes or less from a grandchild. Women, in particular, are also known for their networking skills beyond the family that may lead to a wider range of contacts external to the home.

What may be the impact of these factors? For some, family ties may influence decision making concerning the 'right' place. Whilst for others sharing with non-family members may be more attractive – such as home sharing or co-housing. We need to know more about group and solo living for future generations.

The other important issue that relates to gender – even though it is changing – is transport and access to, and use of, a car. Does the male car user think through the issues of location and accommodation until the day comes when he can no longer drive, and if his wife never drove – what then? This is a different but important issue with regard to maintaining connections with the external environment and for those used to moving may not be thought through.

(c) *Culture* – different cultural and religious practices can also affect the use of space within accommodation. For example, in some groups separation of men's and women's space in the home is the norm:

> There are many degrees of such separation. In a number of Muslim households, women do not enter the men's space when guests are present. In strict Orthodox Jewish households women and men will not socialise together or take part together in religious observance. In many households of other cultures, such as Hindu, Rastafarian and Sikh, the tendency is for men and women to socialise separately.
>
> (National Federation of Housing Associations 1993, p.16)

How do these traditions and customs have an impact on decisions about living arrangements and material environments?

(d) *Income* – income is a crucial factor in relation to living environments affecting location, tenure and housing type. We should also be aware of double and triple jeopardy – older women and older members of minority ethnic groups may form some of the least well-off groups within our society. What does this mean in relation to accommodation where owner occupation has become so dominant? We should recognise the importance of location and the housing market. Who can afford housing and where? Who will be able to afford housing and where?

Leonie Kellaher has drawn our attention to the way in which uniform solutions can be provided for those who cannot buy their way into environments that facilitate continued engagement in later life. But it is also true that supportive housing for older people from minority ethnic groups has seen innovation from which all can learn (Wagner Development Group 1993). The Housing Corporation suggests that black and minority ethnic community-based registered social landlords have been leaders in the 'Housing Plus' initiatives (1998).

With these over-arching characteristics forming a backdrop, I will move on to some of the specific issues Leonie Kellaher raises and reconsider them. I do not find myself disagreeing with the points raised in the paper, but need to use these different types of material in relation to each other.

First, there is the issue of *internal spatial arrangements and under-occupation*. I think this is a crucial issue that links the three areas of materiality, social arrangements and help. I begin here by using my age/life course theme. There are generational issues that permeate people's thinking about space. Caroline Holland has undertaken some research which involved developing housing histories with twenty-five older women. She says this about sharing space: 'Attitudes to, and the general experience of, sharing domestic space with kin and non-kin have changed dramatically during the study period from 1910-1995 as a consequence of widening access to better housing and changing social attitudes.' She quotes two respondents to demonstrate the demise of the extended family:

1930s/40s

I used to sleep with mother, because father was on night work. When dad was at home I had to sleep in my own little bed in their room. When my mother was young, her mother died so she bought the family up, being the eldest daughter. My aunt was the only one of the children that wasn't married, so she lived in rooms upstairs with my grandad. Now there were three rooms upstairs, but they weren't very big, and my brother used to sleep with my grandfather. In those days it was very overcrowded and nobody sort of took any notice did they?

1970s

We stayed with our daughter for a few weeks ... not too long, because her two children wanted a bedroom each, you see. All due respect to us, you know, but ... my son-in-law had to hurry the council to find us a sheltered flat.

(Holland 2001)

In this last quote rather than make do, as seen in the earlier example, the nuclear family sought greater segregation and the older people moved to the sheltered flat. We should therefore be aware that time affects attitudes, which in turn affects decision making.

In this next example I think we can reflect on issues of privacy and the body.

For this older couple from our present study, personal space becomes important as attending to and accommodating the body became a more central part of life. One respondent living in a semi-detached house, said this about bedroom arrangements:

> *Three nice bedrooms, well two are quite large, one's got a shower in it and a sink. The other one ... the main ... I sleep in one, my wife sleeps in the other because once I had this trouble with this thing I used to have to get up three or four times a night and disturbed her. So I've got used to now sleeping in me own double-bed, she sleeps in her own double-bed and that's it, we're quite happy you know. We have a cup of coffee in bed together in the morning and that's it. No problem.*

I think this comment tells us a great deal about the maintenance of self that is supported by environment. Here people are protecting their health and wellbeing through a good nights sleep and yet accommodating affection for each other. Julia Twigg's work on bathing at home is important here (1999) and it is important to relate this work to Leonie's study of space within kitchens and bathrooms.

The connection between self and personal space is also true of my last example, a lady who I visited for many years in Swansea, South Wales when I was a student. She lived in a two-bedroomed house but could no longer climb upstairs and slept on a bed in the front room. I wrote about this some years ago:

> *When I come to visit once a week, Mrs E often sends me upstairs. Last time it was to a wardrobe in the back room where she knew where to locate a handbag which had a letter in it that she wanted to re-read.*

Like the objects that form part of the sitting rooms which Leonie Kellaher's paper describes, this lady is engaging with her environment and using someone else to facilitate this – an intermediary who maintains complexity. It shows us the importance of people and places and I wonder if this is another way of coping with environmental press and making it fit.

Finally, I want to consider that very important topic of the importance of internal and external space. I was reflecting on Graham Rowles' very important study *Prisoners of Space* (1978) when thinking about this. Are people prisoners of space? As the importance of activity within external space declines does the importance of internal space and its differentiation take on a new importance? The more I think about this the more I can see that we still have a lot to learn about the permeability of the boundaries – between rooms; home and garden; home and street; street and neighbourhood. They all reflect levels of engagement, but it is important to realise that motivation within the external world does not have to entail activity – again the word connectedness comes to mind: *'Being a part of but not in.'*

To return to the diversity of living environments and the issue of choice, I feel that for many people opportunities regarding accommodation are constrained in different ways. I am also aware that moving is a stressful time and that maintaining your 'fit' within a space and place presents what Lawton and Nahemow (1973) saw as addressing the challenge of environmental press which also produced engagement. To return to my earlier proposition of 'right space', 'right place', I can also see that what may become the 'wrong' place or the 'wrong' space may create too great a challenge to the maintenance of 'fit'. People may wish to move and this is where they need information to make those decisions. But then I am faced with issues of age discrimination surrounding housing in later life. In a Radio 4 quiz, I heard the comedienne Linda Smith talk of bungalows as 'high rise coffins'(21/01/01), and I still wonder when the estate agents might have these ads in the shop windows. I would argue that when we are able to make all housing more inclusive then we will all have choice and this will see truly inclusive housing (Peace and Holland 2001).

References

Holland, C (2001) Housing Histories: older women's experience of home across the life course, Ph.D Thesis, School of Health and Social Welfare, The Open University.

Housing Corporation (1998) *Black and Minority Ethnic Housing Policy*, London: Housing Corporation.

Lawton, MP and Nahemow, L (1973) Ecology and the ageing process, in C Eisdorfer and MP Lawton (eds) *The Psychology of Adult Development and Ageing*, Washington DC: American Psychological Association.

Peace, SM and Holland CA (eds) (2001) *Inclusive Housing in an Ageing Society: innovative approaches*, Bristol: Policy Press.

66 Malcolm J. Fisk

Rowles, G (1978) *Prisoners of Space? Exploring the Geographical Experiences of Older People*, Boulder CO: Westview Press.

Twigg, J (1999) The spatial ordering of care: public and private in bathing support at home, *Sociology of Health and Illness* 21(4): 381–400.

Wagner Development Group (1993) Black perspectives on residential care, in *Residential Care: positive answers*, London: HMSO, pp. 68–85.

COMMENTARY 2
Malcolm J. Fisk

Leonie Kellaher rightly points to the extraordinary complexity that surrounds the issue of choice. Her exploration into the ways in which people choose to arrange their living spaces (regardless of how they came to be in those particular types of dwellings) gives us some new insights into

- how people relate to their environments;

- how they seek to exercise control over those environments; and

- how both of these are factors in their ability to establish and maintain personal (and, ideally, multidimensional) identities.

To explore such matters she invites us to consider that well known continuum 'from domesticity to institutional living' in a new way, looking at how people use, relate to, and differentiate between spaces; and how these relate to issues such as

- privacy; and

- communality (living with or near other people / households).

The challenge, it seems, is for the older person (in Leonie Kellaher's words) 'to present the self, both to oneself and to others, as a complex multidimensional entity'. She adds, in relation to some kinds of dwellings which she considered, that 'this ... becomes very difficult in the uni-cellular space of the bedsitter/residential room, which cannot easily reveal multiple aspects of personality and experience'.

She is, therefore, at least implicitly critical of some kinds of dwellings (which we can read as nursing and residential homes plus at least some configurations of sheltered housing) that do not provide adequate space within which we can establish and display to others that we are those multidimensional entities, in control of our lives, and able to exercise choices. And she is explicitly critical of the notion that older people will necessarily be content to live in small spaces, especially in view of such small spaces being associated with a reduction in personal privacy. She asserts that 'The virtual elimination of a privacy gradient, with a small world centred on the living room, suggests a view that older people do not inhabit the wider world' and notes that 'older people resist these spatial impositions wherever possible. They hang on to that extra space, they build in complexity where it has been "written out" because they need to do so. They attempt, and in some measure succeed, in re-configuring their space to be more appropriate.'

The notion that there may be a view about that older people do not, or need not, inhabit the wider world is of course ageist. It is small wonder that older people, therefore, resist the 'spatial impositions' dictated by the types of dwellings that are on offer.

It is here that I will start to further consider Leonie Kellaher's question as to how what she calls the 'set of present patterns' of living arrangements gives rise to those 'spatial impositions'; offers or restricts choices; and, by that very fact, represents a suitable context within which older people may explore, develop and flaunt their multidimensionality.

In addition, somehow, somewhere, it seems that Leonie Kellaher believes that there is a 'right fit between dwelling and the self'. What that 'right fit' is, of course, is a matter for debate. But in trying to conclude that debate we should heed her affirmation that we 'need to understand more about patterns of consumption, especially the imaginings whereby people judge if a commodity . . . (including housing) . . . is the right fit'.

So, in an ideal world, regardless of age, we would live in homes that represent that 'right fit'. And that 'right fit' represents a context within which we can be multidimensional.

It follows, therefore, that the ease by which we might exercise housing choices that enable us to progress to that 'right fit', is a key factor in determining the extent to which we can be truly multidimensional and obtain the fulfilment associated with having complex lives over which we can (and can be seen to) exercise control.

I can accept this analysis as long as we bear in mind that the complexity of our lives means that the nature of that 'right fit' can change and may undergo rapid change as a result of different life events. If we argue that life events can be particularly challenging (and sometimes more numerous) for many older people then it follows that the ability for them to exercise choices may be of increasing importance at a time when for many, paradoxically, that ability is reduced.

With this paradox in mind we need to consider the extent to which the range of housing available facilitates the exercising of those choices and the achievement (or at least progress towards the achievement) of that 'right fit'.

Leonie Kellaher says that 'the range of provision that we currently have is quite broad' and, therefore, can be viewed as offering a reasonable choice for older people. She adds, perhaps optimistically, that 'older people are rather good at selecting something that they can work on to fulfil the goal of maintaining their social selves'.

When taking older people as a whole, including those who are reasonably well resourced and active within the private housing market, she is surely right. After all, there is plenty of evidence of older people making choices and moving to different kinds of accommodation both in early retirement and in their later years and, in so doing, perhaps fulfilling dreams and aspirations that had been put 'on hold' during those long years of work and bringing up children.

Most such choices are hardly noticed with those aspirations being satisfied through the sale of a larger property and the purchase of a flat or bungalow. Others are more conspicuous (in the sense that they are commanding more of our attention) and embrace distinctive forms such as private sector sheltered housing, co-housing, retirement communities or park homes.

But the trickiest areas are, of course, those that concern older people who are less well resourced or whose resources have leached away with the years. For them, the aspirations may be similar but the extent to which they can exercise choices is, inevitably, less. Here, using Leonie Kellaher's terms it may be, at best, a matter of 'accepting', 'putting up with' or 'adapting to' certain types of housing. Whereas for exercising choice it might be a matter of 'protesting about' and 'fighting against' certain types of housing when those choices appear to be beginning to be made by others, by housing service providers, by family members, by social workers, by GPs and so on.

In relation to those older people who are less well resourced, therefore, I would say that the range of provision is insufferably narrow, and that what older people want is immensely constrained. As a consequence it is arguably not a matter of 'selecting something that they can work on' but rather 'making do' with something that may be far from the ideal and certainly not a 'right fit'.

Why is this the case? Well, of course, there are issues about the public purse and what should be, or can be, afforded. But space standards (particularly highlighted by Leonie Kellaher) and the configuration of dwellings, notably in the form of sheltered housing, have conspired to treat older people as uni-dimensional.

There is a long tradition of treating older people in this way. It is reflected in the built form that is associated with almshouses and hence may be regarded as having its roots in religious traditions of alms giving. Of course, the giving of alms is a somewhat uni-dimensional activity. As an alms recipient there is little, after all, in the way of negotiation or choice being exercised.

The notion of older people exercising choices on their way to achieving a 'right fit' that enables them to lead full and multidimensional lives is, therefore, substantially compromised in a context where they are, in fact, the recipients of alms in the form of subsidised and specialised and small dwellings that are virtually all that are available to them in the social rented sector.

So older people have to compromise and adapt. In the language of choices, they have no choice but to do so. We can argue that one of those compromises and adaptations relates to space, and with the adaptation to living within restricted spaces, older people must sacrifice their multidimensionality.

To appreciate the implications of this, we need to take a view on what multidimensionality means. At its heart, I suggest, is a complex range of transactions, relationships and exchanges that involve a myriad of people (close and distant), agencies and organisations. And despite the complexity it can be argued that these transactions, relationships and exchanges result in some kind of 'balance' being achieved with the individual freely negotiating his/her position within these. And the fact that the transactions, relationships and exchanges do involve a myriad of people means that it is possible to demonstrate, to flaunt, that multidimensional self to numerous others. Housing or accommodation (whether considered to be a 'right fit' or not) is just one artifact by which this demonstration, or flaunting, is done.

Uni-dimensionality, by contrast, suggests a significant loss in the range of transactions, relationships and exchanges. It also suggests that the balance is upset with the older person no longer being able to freely negotiate his/her position in those transactions, relationships and exchanges.

My hypothesis is, therefore, one that claims that the sacrificing of multidimensionality by many older people is forced and is, at least in part, a consequence of an inadequate range of housing choices.

My view regarding such matters has changed over time as I have gained in experience both as a practitioner (in the public sector delivering housing and social services to older people) and as a researcher, attempting to stand outside that practitioner role and to understand the dynamics associated with needs and choices. The nature of that change in my view has emerged though a gradual realisation that the case for current housing and related service configurations is and was never made.

Social rented housing offers a classic example in sheltered housing. Briefly, the argument for sheltered housing (whenever anyone tried to articulate it) was based on assumptions for which there was little or no evidence. These assumptions are

- that older people need separate housing;
- that older people like to live with their peers;
- that older people prefer to live in smaller dwellings;
- that grouped dwellings foster socialisation and mutual support; and
- that surveillance (in the form of warden services) is necessary for older people.

The evidence for smaller dwellings having been provided for older people (following the assumption that this is what older people want) has already been made very clear from the work described by Leonie Kellaher. If we put this within a broader framework of housing management, the assumption is a very convenient one. It helps, after all, to underpin housing policies that are directed towards reducing what is termed under-occupation, thereby releasing larger dwellings for occupation by families and obtaining what might be viewed as greater efficiency in the housing stock. There are, in other words, ideas held by many housing practitioners about what is the 'right fit' for older people and their dwellings that relates to housing management objectives that might be very much at odds with the needs and aspirations of older people themselves.

While I can be easily persuaded that it might be a good idea for some older people to go in for a certain amount of downsizing, I can recall no one who has ever explained why an older person should be less in need of, for instance, a spare room or a bedroom that is separate from the living room, than a younger person.

Going back to the matter of dimensionality it can be argued that denying older people that spare room, or requiring them to live in dwellings where living rooms are combined with bedrooms, we are reducing their capacity to receive visitors, to cater and to entertain. Worse still in sheltered housing we are obliging older people to socialise with others not of their choosing. We are, in addition, subjecting older people to a regime of surveillance by wardens and support staff whereby their 'status' as service recipients rather than free negotiators is affirmed. In such circumstances, the complex range of transactions, relationships and exchanges which are so necessary if someone is to assert their multidimensionality is at once compromised.

My colleague David Phillips and I made similar points in research that we completed for the Abbeyfield Society (Fisk and Phillips 2001). This followed some very interesting and agonised debates with local Abbeyfield societies about the future of the bedsit. I say agonised because much of the accommodation provision made by such societies is in the form of bedsits, with a perception of their being a continuing 'market' for them.

One particular part of the context of the Abbeyfield research must be understood. This is the importance to Abbeyfield societies of addressing the problems of loneliness and social isolation among older people. We suggested, however, that bedsits might, in fact, make addressing such problems more difficult since residents did not have sufficient space (or rooms) within which they could receive and entertain visitors. Certainly the older people in question were precluded from having people to stay. They could not cook for them, and were generally less able to control the extent of intimacy with or distance from their visitors.

We were arguing, in other words, that space, that the size of dwellings and the number of rooms, can affect the ability of individuals to control at least some of those transactions, relationships and exchanges. Using Leonie Kellaher's terms, a lack of space or an insufficient number of rooms can reduce the ability to assert one's multidimensionality. The conclusion can be none other than bedsits can never represent a 'right fit' if we are to value older people as multidimensional and potentially as full participants in our communities.

Our failure to take account of the multidimensionality of most older people and the consequent limitations in housing choices is, therefore, at best unfortunate and, at worst, has led to a kind of institutional ageism among housing providers. This is, perhaps, most apparent in relation to space standards. But it is also apparent when those other assumptions about sheltered housing are considered.

There is, for instance, little evidence that older people need (or want) separate housing, and where such an aspiration is expressed the motivation is often concerned with personal security rather than a particular need or a specific housing aspiration. We must recognise, furthermore, that by providing separate housing we are denuding communities of their older residents and are almost certainly contributing to their greater exclusion from economic, political and social life of those communities.

There is little evidence that older people prefer to live with their peers. Where research has been brought forward to argue for such a preference it has almost always been done with self-selecting samples of older people who are already living with their peers and for whom there may have been few, if any, alternative choices.

There is little evidence that living in grouped dwellings designated for older people has any especially beneficial effect on socialisation and mutual support any more than living in an ordinary street.

And there is little evidence that surveillance, in the form of wardens, alarm services, daily visits and calls, is necessary for older people. Rather it is suggested that these can infantilise them and foster notions of dependency.

So is genuine choice a reality? The answer must be that genuine choice only exists for some. And the way that we have been responsible for configuring housing provision for those who cannot readily compete in the private housing market has arguably done a great disservice to older people. The challenge now is to reconstruct the service frameworks associated with the current pattern of service provision and to open up housing options in ways that can really begin to offer more choice. The essential preconditions for this are to recognise that

● present social rented housing options (especially in tradi-tional forms of sheltered housing) cannot provide that 'right fit' that responds to peoples' aspirations; and

● older people are multidimensional and need to be appreci-ated as such.

'Special' forms of housing provision (as have characterised social rented housing provision) in a context of limited choices will not provide that 'right fit'. They will continue to foster uni-dimen-sionality rather than multidimensionality and will compromise, therefore, the ability of many older people to retain appropriate personal identities.

What Leonie Kellaher has done is to invite us to recognise the importance of space as we consider new policy and practice frameworks. For the future, however, it must not be a matter of older people 'making do' in a context of the spatial limitations found with some forms of housing. Rather it must be a matter of dramatic reconfigurations of both service frameworks and of the mind-sets of policy makers and practitioners who are concerned with meeting the real needs and aspirations of older people.

Reference

Fisk, MJ and Phillips, D (2001) *New Vistas for Abbeyfield*, St Albans: The Abbeyfield Society.

4 Demography

Living arrangements, receipt of care, residential proximity and housing preferences among older people in Britain and Italy in the 1990s: an overview of trends

Karen Glaser and Cecilia Tomassini

Introduction

The aim of this chapter is to provide a general overview of trends in population ageing as well as an examination of recent trends (in the 1990s) in the living arrangements, receipt of care, residential proximity and housing preferences of older people in Britain, and to provide some comparisons with Italy. This chapter will address the following questions:

1 Is Britain an ageing society?

2 Are older people more likely to live alone, or given past trends in fertility and nuptiality, are they more likely to live with their children in the near future?

3 Is family support for older people declining?

4 Are older people increasingly isolated from family members?

5 Do older people prefer to remain in their own homes and has this changed over time?

Ageing populations

What is an ageing population?

Ageing populations are those in which the proportion of older people is increasing rather than an increase in the absolute numbers (Grundy 1991). Table 4.1 shows, for selected years, the increase in both the proportions and absolute numbers of older people in England and Wales. The proportion of the population aged 65 and over has increased dramatically in England and Wales since 1901. In 1901 the proportion of the population aged 65 and over was around 5 per cent, by 1961 it was 12 per cent, signifying an increase of 153 per cent. The proportion of older people will continue to increase, however, whereas the proportion of the population aged 65 and over increased by 153 per cent between 1901-61 we expect a smaller increase between 1961 and 2011 (i.e. an increase of around 40 per cent). By 2021/2031 we expect a larger increase in the proportion of the population in this age group as the 'baby boom' cohorts (those born in the late 1950s to mid-1960s) begin to age (Table 4.1).

An important future trend is the ageing of the older population itself, which reflects rises in the proportion of the 'oldest old'. For example, the proportion of the population aged 85 and over was only 0.2 per cent in 1901, but by 1961 it had reached 0.7 per cent, an increase of 250 per cent in sixty years. This trend will continue, an increase of 343 per cent is expected in the proportion of those individuals aged 85 and over between 1961 and 2031.

Table 4.1 The older population in England and Wales, 1901–2031

Year	no. (000s)			% aged		
	65–74	75–84	85+	65–74	75–84	85+
1901	992	340	44	4.7	1.3	0.2
1961	3526	1678	309	11.9	4.3	0.7
1991	4506	2810	809	15.9	7.1	1.6
2001	4347	2920	1058	15.7	7.5	2.0
2011	4873	3011	1216	16.6	7.7	2.2
2021	5917	3574	1407	19.2	8.8	2.5
2031	6963	4388	1827	22.7	10.7	3.1

Source: 1901–1961 Table in *House Magazine*, June 24, 1991, p.19.
1991 Table 1.5 in *Population Trends* 100, 2000, p. 53.
2001–2031 GAD, 1998-based national population projections
(http://www.gad.gov.uk/population/1998/engwal/popew98.html)

What are the causes of population ageing?

Population ageing is the result of sustained downward trends in fertility (Grundy 1991). Falling fertility leads to fewer young people in the population and hence a rise in the proportion who are old. In England and Wales the total fertility rate (TFR)[1] was 5 at the end of the nineteenth century; decreased to a low of 1.7 in 1933; rose again during the post-War baby boom (achieving a TFR of 2.8 in 1947); reached a high during the baby boom of the 1960s (reaching a TFR of nearly 3 in 1964); and has continued to decline steadily ever since (the TFR is currently 1.7) (Armitage and Babb 1996, Ruddock *et al.* 1998). However, changes in mortality are also an important factor, especially in societies that already have low fertility and mortality levels. Mortality decline at older ages is particularly important for the ageing of the older population itself, i.e. increases in the proportion of the 'oldest old'.

The greying of the world's population

Population ageing is not just a British phenomenon, it is a global trend (Kinsella and Velkoff 2001, UN 1999). Most countries in the world have experienced a significant drop in fertility which has resulted in quite dramatic increases in the proportion of the older population. Europe is currently the world's oldest region, and Southern European countries, along with some Eastern European countries as well as a number of the former Soviet Republics, have the highest proportion of older people in Europe (Kinsella and Velkoff 2001). In fact, Italy is currently the world's oldest country (Kinsella and Velkoff 2001). This is because fertility is lower in these countries, and many have sustained low fertility levels over a long period of time (e.g. Italy has experienced low fertility since the 1970s), leading to higher proportions of the population aged 65 and over.

Background

Population ageing has significant social and financial implications for families and governments, and this has led to considerable interest in the future care needs of older people and the availability of family support. One way to examine family support is to study the living arrangements of older people. Given that the availability of help from within the household influences demand for assistance from outside, including state

---

1 The TFR is a period measure of fertility and refers to the number of children women could expect to have given age-specific levels of fertility at a specific point in time.

services, understanding the nature and determinants of living arrangements among older individuals is important from a policy perspective (Arber *et al.* 1988).

Following the post-World War II period there has been a dramatic rise in the proportions of older people living alone in Britain, as well as in other industrialised countries (Kobrin 1976, Pampel 1992, Sundström 1994). However, recent evidence shows a slowdown, and in some cases a reversal, in this trend (Macunovich *et al.* 1995, Tomassini and Wolf 2000). This study uses the General Household Survey (1991, 1994, 1998) and the British Household Panel Survey (1991, 1994, 1998) to compare recent trends in the household composition of older people in Britain with those in Italy (using the 1990, 1994 and 1998 Indagine Multiscopo sulle Famiglie), where researchers have demonstrated a decrease in solitary living in the 1990s (Tomassini and Wolf 2000).

Rises in solitary living have also led to concerns regarding increased reliance on state assistance for frail older people, as studies have found that the allocation of formal care (e.g., home help) was significantly more likely among older people who lived alone than those who were married (Arber *et al.* 1988). Therefore, this study also examines trends in the receipt of care among older people in Britain, using the 1991, 1994 and 1998 General Household Survey (GHS). In addition, as trends in the proximity of parents and their children will clearly affect the availability of family support, this study presents some data from the British Social Attitudes Survey (1986, 1995) regarding residential proximity. Finally, this study examines trends in the mobility and housing preferences of older people using data from the British Household Panel Survey (1991, 1994, 1998).

Data

British Household Panel Survey (BHPS)

The British Household Panel Survey (BHPS) was used to examine changes in living arrangements and housing preferences among older people in the same three survey years as were used in the analysis of the GHS (1991, 1994, 1998). The BHPS is an annual survey which began in 1991 and interviewed every adult household member (16+) of a nationally representative sample of around 5,000 private households (Taylor *et al.* 2001). This resulted in a sample size of about 10,000 individuals for each survey. The

BHPS is a longitudinal survey, therefore the same individuals are re-interviewed each year along with any new household members (Taylor *et al.* 2001). Additional sub-samples were added to the BHPS in 1997 and 1999. In the 1997 survey a sub-sample of 1,000 households from the British European Community Household Panel (ECHP) was added (Taylor *et al.* 2001). The figures in this study based on the BHPS have been weighted to adjust for the ECHP sub-sample as well as for non-response. The advantage of the BHPS, in contrast to the GHS, is that it can provide information on transitions.[2] The BHPS, however, can also be used cross-sectionally to examine changes over time in both behaviour and attitudes. Information on the living arrangements of older people is derived from the household schedules provided for each survey wave. The BHPS also contains attitudinal data. While the British Social Attitudes Survey (BSAS) is the predominate source of attitudinal data in Britain, its sample sizes are quite small at older ages (the BSAS are annual attitudinal surveys, begun in 1983, with a total of around 3,500 respondents). Since the survey started in 1991 the BHPS has included attitudinal questions on whether respondents would prefer to move house, the reasons for this preference, and whether or not respondents like their present neighbourhood. Questions on housing satisfaction have only been asked since 1996.

General Household Survey (GHS)

The General Household Survey (GHS) was used to analyse trends in living arrangements and receipt of care among older people in Britain. The GHS is a continuous household survey which has run every year since 1971, with the exception of 1997 and 1999 (Bridgwood *et al.* 2000). The survey's sample size is around 18,000 people aged 16 and over, drawn from the general population resident in private households in Britain. This study focuses on the surveys conducted in 1991, 1994, and 1998 which included a module of questions asked to people aged 65 and over concerning their living circumstances, health, ability to manage a selection of self-care and domestic tasks, as well as their use of health and personal social services (Bridgwood *et al.* 2000). The living arrangements of older people was determined from the household

---

2 The BHPS has been used to look at transitions in the living arrangements of older people (see Evandrou *et al.* 2001).

information and family information given in the GHS. Receipt of care was determined from the set of questions concerning the respondent's ability to manage a series of activities and tasks. These questions measured Activities of Daily Living (ADLs), defined as those tasks essential to survival without help (e.g. walking out of doors and down the road; walking up and down stairs; getting around the house (on the level); getting to the toilet; getting in and out of bed; feeding; washing face and hands; dressing and undressing).[3] Individuals who could only manage the ADL activities with help from someone else were asked who provided that assistance, and for the 1994 and 1998 surveys it was also possible to distinguish those who could not manage the task at all (and were not receiving help from someone else).

Based on this information a summary variable was created indicating whether respondents could manage all the ADL activities described on their own; whether they received help with one or more of the ADL tasks from family members only; whether they received help from either a combination of family and non-family members or non-family members only; or whether they were not able to manage at all one or more of the ADL tasks, and were not receiving help from either family or non-family sources. The overall measure has been made as comparable across surveys as possible, although this was difficult given differences in the question wording for the various ADL activities between the surveys.

Although the Family Resources Survey (FRS) is based on a larger sample size (the 1998 survey interviewed 40,500 adults) and also collects information on those receiving help, GHS data provided a more complete picture of the recipient of informal care as the questions on care receipt in the FRS were only asked on the 'household schedule' and were not asked of individual respondents (so that the person actually receiving the care may not have been directly addressed) (Department of Social Security 2000).

British Social Attitude Surveys (BSAS)

The British Social Attitudes Surveys (BSAS) is a series of annual surveys carried out in Great Britain between 1983 and 2000 (the

---

3 Questions concerning whether the respondent was able to bathe, shower, or wash him/herself all over were included in the 1994 and 1998 GHS, but not in the 1991 GHS. Therefore these measures were excluded from the overall ADL measure used in this analysis.

latest year for which data is currently available), except for the years 1988 and 1992. The survey is undertaken by Social and Community Planning Research (SCPR). Based on the General Social Survey in the US, the BSAS is designed to monitor trends in attitudes (Lilley *et al.* 1997). The BSAS is an annual cross-sectional survey of a representative sample of adults aged 18 and over living in private households in Great Britain (Lilley *et al.* 1997). Only one adult per household is interviewed. In 1983 some 1,700 individuals were interviewed, between 1986 and 1993 the sample size was around 3,000 and more recently the sample size has increased to around 3,500 (Lilley *et al.* 1997).

As few surveys contain data on the proximity between parents and children,[4] this study presents previously published and unpublished data on proximity from the 1986 and 1995 BSAS. The BSAS consist of various parts, the core questionnaire which is put to all respondents, non-core questions which are only asked of a sample of respondents, and self-completion question-naires which are also only administered to some of the sample. Questions concerning proximity were in the self-completion questionnaire which respondents were asked to fill in and which were then collected by the interviewer. The weights applied to the 1995 BSAS reflect the 'relative selection probabilities of the individual at the three main stages of selection: address, house-hold and individual' (Lilley *et al.* 1997).

Indagine Multiscopo sulle Famiglie (Italy)

The analysis used data from the Indagine Multiscopo sulle Famiglie, a survey carried out every year on the private house-hold population of Italy. The unit of the sample is the 'de facto' household selected from the Register of Population. A two-stage probability sampling design at the municipal and household level was employed. A wide variety of topics are covered by the survey, including questions on household structure, demo-graphic background, housing, area of residence, health status and leisure time. The survey has a total sample size of around 60,000 respondents.

---

4 The 1988/89 and 1994 ONS Retirement Survey included data on proximity
   between parents and children (questions referred to nearest child). In the
   1999 ONS Omnibus survey questions on proximity between parents and
   children referred to proximity to the eldest child (see Grundy *et al.* 1999).

Trends in the living arrangements of older people

Living arrangements up to 1991: an overview

The most important change in the living arrangements of the older population in Britain in the post-World War II period was the large increase in the proportions living alone (Grundy 1996, Wall 1995). Other industrialised nations, such as the US and Japan, have also experienced a similar trend (Kramarow 1995, Ogawa and Retherford 1997, Pampel 1992, Sundström 1994, Wolf 1995). This increase in the proportion of older people living alone has been accompanied by a general decline in the number of individuals living with relatives, particularly children, or non-related individuals (Grundy 2000, Keilman 1987, Kobrin 1976, Murphy and Berrington 1993, van Solinge 1994, Wall 1995).

While historically in Britain it was never common for older people to live with their children, more older persons in pre-industrial times lived with a child than they do today (Wall 1995). About 40 per cent of older men and one third of older women lived with a child in the pre-industrial communities studied by Wall (Wall 1995). By contrast, never more than around 5 per cent of men, and 16 per cent of women aged 65 years and over, lived alone (Wall 1995). The percentage of older people living alone remained fairly constant until the 1960s, when the percentage rose dramatically. Data from the ONS Longitudinal Study showed that between 1971 and 1991 the percentage of men aged 65 and over living alone increased from 13 to 19 per cent, and for women from 34 to 43 per cent (Grundy 1996).

Some of the changes responsible for this trend toward greater residential independence among older people, such as greater financial independence and possible improvements in health, are positive developments which may enable more older individuals to meet aspirations for 'intimacy at a distance' rather than having to co-reside with family members (Grundy 1997, McGarry and Schoeni 2000). There are, however, other factors which have also had an impact on the household composition of older people, such as low fertility rates among older cohorts, which has reduced the number of kin with whom older people can co-reside; increasing female employment, which may have reduced women's willingness to look after older relatives; and rises in divorce and single motherhood, which may have weakened family ties and hence perceptions of felt obligation toward older relatives (Glaser 1997).

Living arrangements 1990s: recent evidence

This trend toward solitary living among the older population in Britain and other industrialised nations has been well established in the literature. Recent work in the US and Italy, however, has shown a reversal of these earlier trends (Macunovich *et al.* 1995, Tomassini and Wolf 2000). This reversal has been attributed to the following factors: 1) rises in the proportions of older people living in a couple only household, due to both the increased survivorship of partners, and rises in the proportions married among the young-old age groups; 2) increases in the availability of kin with whom older people may co-reside, a result of the ageing of the baby boomer's parents; and 3) later ages at leaving the parental home among the younger generation, a result of longer periods of education, later marriage and a later stable working career.

Changes in survivorship and marital status

Spouse availability is an important influence on living arrangements, and is determined in large measure by past first marriage patterns and the incidence and duration of widowhood and divorce (Murphy and Grundy 1994). High proportions of women in the cohorts of survivors who now comprise the oldest old never married. Marriage rates rose in the post-War period so that the proportions married are currently higher among the young-old population than among the oldest old (Grundy 1999). For example, 12 per cent of women born in 1910 never married compared with only 5 per cent of those born in 1936 (Haskey 1993, ONS 1999).

Co-residence with a spouse is also strongly influenced by the prevalence of widowhood in later life. Women, in general, spend a greater proportion of their lives as widows given their higher survival rates when compared with those of men and the common pattern of marrying older men. Continuing improvements in life expectancy have meant that women currently spend a prolonged period as widows and are therefore more likely to end up living alone (Hareven 1992). On the other hand, after a century or more in which women's mortality declined more than that of men, there have recently been greater improvements in male than female mortality which has meant that more young-old women are able to live with a spouse for longer (Grundy 1998). Men are more likely to live with a spouse than women at older ages given the higher survival rates of women and the fact that men are more likely to marry younger partners than women.

Previous research using the ONS Longitudinal Study showed that while the proportions of older people living alone rose between 1971 and 1991, the percentage living in a couple also increased (Grundy 1996).

Changes in kin availability

Numerous studies have demonstrated that individuals with more children are less likely to live alone at older ages than those with fewer children (Mutchler 1992, Wolf 1994). In addition, kin availability is an important predictor of changes over time in the pattern of solitary living among older women (Wolf 1995). In Western Europe, women born before the mid-1920s often had fewer children than women born in the 1930s and 1940s (see Table 4.2 for Britain and Italy). Lower fertility combined with higher levels of childlessness may, in part, account for the higher prevalence of solitary living amongst the oldest old.

Table 4.2 Average achieved family size (by age 45) by year of birth: Britain and Italy

Birth cohort	Average number of liveborn children per woman
Britain	
1921	2.1
1935	2.4
Italy	
1921	2.4
1935	2.3

GB: OPCS. *Birth Statistics. Review of the Registrar on Births and Patterns of Family Building in England and Wales*, 1990. London: HMSO, 1992.
I: ISTAT. (1997) 'La fecondità nelle regioni italiane-Analisi per coorti – Anni 1952–1995'.

Recent research in the US shows that the proportion of young-old widowed women living alone has decreased, whereas there has been an increase in solitary living among older cohorts of widowed women (i.e., those aged 80 years and over) (Macunovich *et al.* 1995). The trend among young older widows toward increased co-residence with children in the US is thought to be due, in large part, to higher fertility achieved during the 'baby boom'. Italy, like the US, has also seen a decline in the percentage of young-old unmarried women living alone (i.e., the never-married, widowed and divorced) (Tomassini and Wolf 2000). In both studies it is suggested that as the mothers of the 'baby boom' generation age we may witness declines in the proportion of older women living alone, due to the increased availability of kin with whom they may co-reside.

Household composition of older people in Britain and Italy

Table 4.3a shows the proportions of men and women aged 65 years and over by household composition in Britain. The GHS and BHPS both show that the proportions of men living alone has stabilised in the 1990s, whereas the proportions living with a spouse have increased. In addition, the proportion of older individuals living with children or in 'other' types of households has declined. Trends for women are similar to those for men.

Table 4.3b shows trends in the living arrangements among older people in Italy. Like Britain, there has been a slowdown in the trend toward solitary living although there is a less pronounced trend toward living in a couple only. Living with others has increased slightly between 1994 and 1998 especially among men.

Table 4.4 shows trends in the living arrangements of unmarried women in Britain and in Italy as it appears to be for this group that the reversal in the trend in solitary living appears the most pronounced. In Britain, there has been a small increase in the proportions living alone, whereas in Italy the percentage living alone decreased between 1991 and 1998. In Britain, the percentage of unmarried women living with children has remained stable between 1994 and 1998, compared with Italy where the percentage of unmarried women living with children has declined slightly. In Britain the percentage of unmarried women living with others (largely siblings) has declined, whereas in Italy the percentage in this group has increased.

Table 4.3a Trends in the living arrangements of older people aged 65 years and over: General Household Survey (1991, 1994, 1998) and British Household Panel Survey (1991, 1994, 1998), Britain

Living arrangement	Men			Women		
	1991 (%)	1994 (%)	1998 (%)	1991 (%)	1994 (%)	1998 (%)
GHS						
Living alone	23.2	23.5	23.3	47.8	47.6	45.6
Couple only	61.9	60.9	64.6	35.2	34.9	40.6
Couple and children only	7.0	6.6	5.3	2.8	2.7	2.1
Other	7.9	9.0	6.8	14.2	14.8	11.7
N	1763	1505	1412	2500	2125	1824
BHPS						
Living alone	21.3	24.8	24.1	49.7	55.8	51.4
Couple only	61.7	62.5	63.1	33.8	32.6	36.8
Couple and children only	8.1	6.0	6.0	3.5	2.1	2.5
Other	8.9	6.7	6.7	13.1	9.6	9.3
N (weighted)	800	784	986	1192	1128	1340

Note: For the GHS these tabulations are based on all older individuals in the survey not just those who answered the module of questions addressed to those aged 65 and over.

Table 4.3b Trends in the living arrangements of older people aged 65 years and over: Indagine Multiscopo, Italy

Living arrangement	Men			Women		
	1991 (%)	1994 (%)	1998 (%)	1991 (%)	1994 (%)	1998 (%)
GHS						
Living alone	11.7	13.0	12.4	40.2	36.9	36.8
Couple only	54.8	51.6	51.2	27.6	28.8	28.6
Couple and children only	26.4	28.1	24.6	9.1	10.5	9.8
Other	7.2	7.3	11.8	23.1	23.8	24.6
N (weighted)	4148	2150	3484	5226	4900	4488

Table 4.4 Trends in the living arrangements of unmarried women aged 65 years and over: General Household Survey (1991, 1994, 1998), Britain and Indagine Multiscopo, Italy

	1991	1994	1998
Britain			
Living alone	78.3	78.5	81.4
With children	15.9	15.3	15.1
With others	5.8	6.2	3.5
N	1519	1278	1021
Italy			
Living alone	62.8	60.0	61.1
With children	28.9	30.1	29.3
With others	8.2	9.9	9.6
N	3044	3000	2576

Trends in receipt of care among older people

The increase in the proportion of older people living alone has led to concerns about the future of family care for older people. Although the needs of carers were explicitly recognised in the community care reforms in Britain in the 1990s (NHS and Community Care Act 1990, and the Carers Recognition and Services Act 1995), it remains unclear what impact these reforms have had on informal carers. Although the intention of the reforms was to address inadequate service provision, recent evidence shows a decline in the level of service support for those individuals who have an informal carer (Rowlands 1998). However, only a small portion of care is provided by public social services in most industrial societies, the great majority of the care received by older people continues to be provided by family members including other older people, particularly spouses (Arber and Ginn 1993, Walker 1995). The norm of family care, however, may not be the ideal situation for either the caregiver or recipient. There is growing evidence to suggest that older people may prefer professional assistance in some circumstances, especially with tasks such as personal care (Daatland 1990). In the 1997 ONS Omnibus Survey, 40 per cent of men and 33 per cent of women aged 65 years and over stated that they would prefer a mixture of family support and professional care in their own home if in the future they were no longer able to manage on their own (Glaser *et al.* 1998). In addition, 28 per cent of women and 23 per cent of men aged 65 and over stated that they would prefer only the assistance of a professional carer in their home in such a situation (Glaser *et al.* 1998).

Trends in the receipt of care for ADL activities among older people, Britain

Table 4.5 shows that, with the exception of Denmark, in most countries in the European Union (selected countries shown), the great majority of care received by older people is provided by family members. A small proportion of care is provided by public social services at young-old ages, although this proportion increases with age (Glaser *et al.* 1998).

Table 4.5 'Who gives you regular help or assistance?' Among respondents who get regular help or assistance with personal care or household tasks because they find it difficult to do these by themselves, persons aged 65 and over

Gender and who receive help from	Great Britain	Denmark	Netherlands	Italy
Men				
Family only	42.5	23.5	28.8	82.7
Non-family only	5.1	5.1	7.3	3.6
Paid help only	6.3	13.5	27.1	11.5
Public social service only[a]	13.7	32.1	23.5	2.2
Mix	25.8	25.8	13.3	0.0
N	31	30	53	39
Women				
Family only	44.6	12.3	26.1	67.3
Non-family only	6.7	0.8	15.7	1.9
Paid help only	9.0	3.8	21.0	19.2
Public social service only[a]	10.6	46.9	25.1	1.7
Mix	10.0	36.3	12.1	10.0
N	55	66	90	57

[a] Includes few who receive help from someone from a voluntary organisation or charity group.
Source: 1992 *Eurobarometer* 37(2).

Table 4.6 shows the proportion of men and women aged 65 and over in Britain who were receiving care for ADL activities. It is necessary to be cautious in interpreting the trends in Table 4.6 as the ADL question wording differed across the GHS surveys. In general, the proportions who could manage on their own increased between 1991 and 1998, whereas the proportions who could not manage at all decreased between 1994 and 1998. A higher proportion of individuals received help from family members than from other sources. The ratio of family help to family and/or non-family help, however, increased between 1994 and 1998, with the receipt of help in 1998 more likely to come solely from family sources than in 1994.

Table 4.6 Trends in the receipt of care for ADL activities among individuals aged 65 years and over: General Household Survey (1991, 1994, 1998), Britain

Receipt of care	Men			Women		
	1991 (%)	1994 (%)	1998 (%)	1991 (%)	1994 (%)	1998 (%)
Manage on own	92.0	89.2	92.3	85.0	80.0	83.0
Family only help	5.7	5.6	4.3	9.9	9.5	8.3
Family and non-family help[a]	2.3	0.6	0.8	5.1	2.2	3.2
Cannot manage at all	–	4.6	2.7	–	8.3	5.6
N	1555	1441	1336	2176	2036	1745

[a] Includes individuals receiving both family and non-family help as well as those receiving only non-family help.

Trends in proximity between older people and their children

If the needs of frail older people cannot be met from within the household it is likely that these needs will be met by kin living in close proximity. For this reason the issue of residential proximity of older people to their kin has become increasingly important (Wolf 1994). Furthermore, as nearby kin may be able to provide similar support to co-resident kin (Mancini and Bleiszner 1989), declines in co-residence may imply little or no loss of potential family support.

Research on the spatial proximity of older people and their kin is largely American (Clark and Wolf 1992, Clark *et al.* 1994, Lin and Rogerson 1995), although there have been some European studies (Glaser and Tomassini 2000, Shelton and Grundy 2000,Warnes 1986). Although the proportion of older people who live close to a child has decreased over time, a significant proportion continue to remain in close proximity to at least one child (Grundy *et al.* 1999, Jarvis 1993). Evidence from the 1999 ONS Omnibus Survey shows that even for men and women aged 70 to 79 years, over 40 per cent lived within 30 minutes of their non-resident eldest child (Grundy *et al.* 1999). Changes over time in residential proximity between parents and children are likely to be the result of increases in job related mobility, and greater personal mobility due to rises in car ownership, better roads, and increased ease of communication through alternative means such as the telephone or computers (Warnes 1986).

Frequency of face-to-face contact has decreased although it still remains high. The 1999 ONS Omnibus Survey showed that over 40 per cent of men and women saw their eldest child at least once a week (Grundy *et al.* 1999).

Trends in residential proximity: Britain

Table 4.7 shows that there has been a decrease in proximity between older parents and their children since the 1960s. However, even in 1995, 45 per cent of people aged 65 had their closest child living within 10-15 minutes travel time. Studies which have examined the proximity of adult children to their parents found no change over time between 1986 and 1995 once other factors were controlled for, but they did find a change between 1995 and 1999, an increase rather than a decrease in proximity between adult children and their parents (Shelton and Grundy 2000).

Table 4.7 Contacts and proximity of older people with kin, people aged 65 and over, Britain 1962, 1986, 1995

Frequency	1962 (%)	1986 (%)	1995 (%)
Seeing child within a week	86	73	67
Seeing sibling within a week	35	23	19
Child lives within 10-15 minutes travel[a]	66	40[b]	45

[a]Includes co-resident children.
[b]In the 1986 BSAS respondents were asked separately about proximity to sons and daughters whereas in the 1995 BSAS respondents were asked about the son or daughter they had the most contact with.
Source: 1962 Shanas, E, Townsend, P, Wedderburn, D, Friis, H, Milhøj, P and Stehower, J (1968) *Old People in Three Industrial Societies*, London: Routledge, Kegan Paul.
1986 Jarvis, C (1993). *Family and Friends in Old Age, and the Implications for Informal Support: evidence from the British Social Attitudes Survey of 1986*, Working Paper No. 6, London: Age Concern Institute of Gerontology.
1995 Author's calculations from 1995 British Social Attitudes Survey (BSAS).

Trends in living arrangements and housing preferences

It is well established that rates of geographical mobility among older people are lower than among younger adults. Most older people do not migrate, and those who do tend to move only short distances (Warnes 1996). For example, only 4 per cent of individuals aged 60 and over had moved in the year prior to the 1991 British Census compared with 10 per cent for all age groups (Warnes 1996). Some countries show a distinct trend in the migration pattern of older individuals, with migration peaking around retirement age, and then again in later old age, the latter trend being associated with disability related migration (Rogers 1988).

Given the dramatic changes in the living arrangements of older people which occurred since the post-World War II period (i.e., rises in the proportions living alone and decreases in proportion living with kin), earlier work in Britain sought to examine changes in the relationship between household change and migration since the 1970s (1971-81 and 1981-91) using the ONS Longitudinal Study. This work showed surprisingly little change in migration patterns among those aged 65 and over in England and Wales between the two time periods (Glaser and Grundy 1998). Among those aged 75 and over this appeared, in part, to reflect reduced movement associated with transitions from one type of private household to another (in short, fewer people moving to live with relatives) which offset the increased mobility associated with higher transition rates from private to non-private households in the 1980s.

Using data from the BSAS (1985, 1986, 1991),[5] earlier work examined trends in whether or not individuals would prefer to remain in their present homes if given a free choice. This work showed little change over time in the proportions who preferred to remain in their present accommodation, although there was a small increase in the percentage who reported that they would like to stay in their present homes (Glaser *et al.* 1998). In the BSAS respondents who reported that they would prefer to move were not asked their reasons for this preference. Previous

---

5   The question in the BSAS was 'If you had a free choice, would you choose to stay in your present home, or would you choose to move out?' This question was asked again in the 1997 and 1998 BSAS.

research, also using the BSAS, reported high levels of satisfaction among respondents with their present accommodation.[6] In general, individuals in the older age groups expressed greater satisfaction with their present accommodation than their younger counterparts (Glaser *et al.* 1998).

Ford and Warnes's (1995) work, based on the Residential Mobility in Later Life (MILL) survey which contained a sample of households with at least one individual aged 60 years or over from the Southeast region, also found a positive relationship between age and housing satisfaction, which rose steadily from age 65-69 to age 85 and over. Unlike the BSAS, which did not ask respondents what they did not like about their homes, the MILL survey measured housing dissatisfaction by asking respondents to name up to three features which they would most like to change about their dwellings (Warnes and Ford 1995). Respondents cited the high running cost of their home (30 per cent), the work load of the garden (27 per cent), the risk of entry to burglars or intruders (24 per cent), and the work load of the house (17 per cent) as features they would most like to improve (Warnes and Ford 1995). Questions concerning respondents' neighbourhoods in the BSAS varied greatly by year and were largely concerned with perceptions of crime (e.g. whether, in the area in which they lived, respondents felt safe walking after dark, whether it was common for people's homes to be burgled or for deliberate damage to be done by vandals, etc). The BSAS, as well as other surveys such as the British Crime survey, show that older people are far more likely to feel unsafe in their local areas than their younger counterparts. In fact, older people are less at risk of violence than younger people, in part, because they are less likely to leave home. In 1995 only 1 per cent of individuals aged 60 years and over were a victim of a contact crime compared with 13 per cent of those aged 16-29 (Mirrlees-Black *et al.* 1996). It has been hypothesised that older people are more likely to report feeling unsafe in their local areas than younger individuals as these anxieties may also encompass fear of mishaps and accidents as well as crime (Mirrlees-Black *et al.* 1996).

---

6 The question of housing satisfaction in the BSAS was 'In general, how satisfied or dissatisfied are you with your own (house/flat)?' Questions on housing satisfaction in the BSAS have been asked every year from 1983 to 1991 (with the exception of 1984).

Trends in mobility and housing preferences: Britain

This section examines mobility data in the BHPS (1991, 1994, 1998), whether individuals would prefer to move, and reasons for this preference (which is not available in the BSAS), as well as reported satisfaction with housing and their neighbourhood.[7]

Table 4.8 shows the proportion of men and women aged 65 and over who moved location in the year prior to the surveys in 1994 and 1998. The proportion of men and women who moved remained fairly small in the mid to late 1990s. Table 4.9 shows that the majority of men and women aged 65 years and over would prefer to stay in their present home, and that this proportion has increased over time. For example, among men aged 65 and over, 71 per cent preferred to stay in their own home in 1991 compared with 78 per cent in 1998. Those who reported that they would prefer to move house were asked for their reasons. Table 4.10 shows no consistent pattern in the reasons given, although for all three years women were significantly more likely than men to give family or health related reasons for wanting to move, whereas men were more likely to give reasons relating to the nature of the accommodation. Both men and women consistently reported satisfaction with their present neighbourhood over time (Table 4.11). Housing satisfaction was only asked in 1998 and women were significantly more likely to report higher levels of satisfaction with their accommodation than men (Table 4.11).

Table 4.12 shows living arrangements by housing preference for men and women. Among women in all three selected years of the BHPS there was a consistent significant relationship between living arrangement and housing preference, with women living with others more likely to report a preference to move home than women living alone.

---

7 The Survey of English Housing does not ask respondents about whether they would prefer to move and reasons for this preference. The survey does ask respondents who moved within the three years prior to the survey the reasons for the move.

Table 4.8 Percentage of respondents aged 65 years and over who moved location since last wave, by gender and year, BHPS, Britain

	Men			Women		
	1991 (%)	*1994 (%)*	*1998 (%)*	*1991 (%)*	*1994 (%)*	*1998 (%)*
Mover status (98)						
Non-mover	–	96.5	98.4	–	96.6	97.1
Mover	–	3.5	1.6	–	3.4	2.9
N (weighted)	–	784	986	–	1128	1340

Table 4.9 'If you could choose, would you stay here in your present home or would you prefer to move somewhere else?', by gender and year, BHPS, Britain

	Men			Women		
	1991 (%)	*1994 (%)*	*1998 (%)*	*1991 (%)*	*1994 (%)*	*1998 (%)*
Prefers to move house (91, 94)						
Stay here	70.8	73.4	77.6	77.6	77.6	80.8
Prefer to move	28.5	26.1	21.5	21.6	21.2	18.3
Don't know	0.8	0.5	0.9	0.8	1.2	0.9
N (weighted)	799	784	986	1192	1128	1340

Table 4.10 'What is the main reason why you would prefer to move?', among those who would prefer to move somewhere else by gender and year, BHPS, Britain

Receipt of care	Men			Women		
	1991 (%)	*1994 (%)*	*1998 (%)*	*1991 (%)*	*1994 (%)*	*1998 (%)*
Why would prefer to move house						
Accommodation	21.9	25.3	30.9	31.0	35.5	29.6
Health/family	16.8	16.9	10.7	21.5	22.1	23.7
Environment	42.0	53.5	47.1	36.7	36.6	40.5
Other	19.3	4.3	11.2	10.8	5.8	6.2
N (weighted)	226	205	210	251	237	246

Table 4.11 'Overall, do you like living in this neighbourhood?' and 'How dissatisfied or satisfied are you with your house/flat', by gender and year, BHPS, Britain

	Men			Women		
	1991 (%)	1994 (%)	1998 (%)	1991 (%)	1994 (%)	1998 (%)
Like present neighbourhood						
Yes	92.7	92.7	94.0	90.9	91.0	93.2
No	6.4	6.9	5.0	8.8	8.3	6.5
Don'know	0.9	0.5	1.0	0.4	0.7	0.3
N (weighted)	800	781	984	1192	1127	1337
Satisfaction with house/flat						
Completely satisfied	–	–	49.8	–	–	56.0
Middle	–	–	48.5	–	–	43.2
Not satisfied	–	–	1.8	–	–	0.8
N (weighted)			962			1283

Table 4.12 Living arrangement and housing preference by gender and year, BHPS, Britain

Lliving arrangement and housing preference	Men			Women		
	1991 (%)	1994[b] (%)	1998 (%)	1991[a] (%)	1994[c] (%)	1998[d] (%)
Living alone						
Housing preference						
Prefers to stay here	74.0	79.5	81.0	81.1	81.7	83.5
Prefers to move	24.3	19.3	17.4	18.0	16.6	15.2
Don't know	1.8	1.2	1.6	0.9	1.7	1.3
N (weighted)	170	195	238	592	629	689
Living with others						
Housing preference						
Prefers to stay here	69.9	71.4	76.5	74.1	72.6	78.0
Prefers to move	29.6	28.4	22.8	25.2	26.9	21.7
Don't know	0.5	0.2	0.7	0.8	0.5	0.4
N (weighted)	629	589	748	600	498	651

[a] $\chi^2=9.2$; df=2, p<.05
[b] $\chi^2=9.0$; df=2; p<.05
[c] $\chi^2=20.4$; df=2; p<.01
[d] $\chi^2=12.1$; df=2; p<.01

Summary and discussion

Given continuing low fertility levels in Britain and Italy, as well as improvements in mortality at the oldest ages, there is no doubt that population ageing will continue. For the 1990s, there appeared to be a slowdown in the proportions of older people living alone, however, there may be a rise in the future. Family continues to be the main provider of care to frail older people. GHS data shows a rise in the share of family to non-family care in the 1990s. Proximity between parents and children has decreased over time, but a high proportion continue to live close to a child and to have frequent contact. Older individuals are generally satisfied with their housing and neighbourhood and would prefer to remain in their own homes. However, it is likely that changes in housing preferences will occur as individuals age and their circumstances change (e.g. bereavement, poor health, etc). The relationship between changes in individual circumstance and preferences would best be captured using longitudinal rather than cross-sectional data. Although such a dataset focusing specifically on older people is not yet available it is hoped that the English Longitudinal Study of Ageing, launched in 2000 and covering a wide range of topics, will be able to bridge this gap.

Acknowledgement

We are grateful to the Data Archive at the University of Essex for providing access to the following surveys: the British Social Attitudes Survey, the Eurobarometer Survey, the General Household Survey, and the British Household Survey. All responsibility for the analysis and interpretation of data reported here rests with the authors.

References

Arber, S, Gilbert, GN and Evandrou, M (1988) Gender, household composition and receipt of domiciliary services by elderly disabled people, *Journal of Social Policy* 17: 153–175.
Arber, S and Ginn, J (1993) Gender and inequalities in health in later life, *Social Science and Medicine* 36: 33–46.
Armitage, B and Babb, P (1996) Population Review: (4) Trends in fertility, *Population Trends* 84: 7–13.
Bridgwood, A, Lilly, R, Thomas, M, Bacon, J, Sykes, W and Morris, S

(2000) *Living in Britain: results from the 1998 General Household Survey*, London: The Stationery Office.

Clark, RL and Wolf, DA (1992) Proximity of children and elderly migration, in A Rogers (ed.) *Elderly Migration and Population Redistribution: a comparative study*, London: Belhaven Press.

Clark, RL, Wolf, DA and Schulte, M (1994, May 5-7) Apart and Together: transitions between coresidence, propinquity, and distance among parents and their children. Paper presented at the Annual Meetings of the Population Association of America, Miami, Florida.

Daatland, SO (1990) What are families for? On family solidarity and preference for help, *Ageing and Society* 10: 1–15.

Department of Social Security (2000) *Family Resources Survey Great Britain 1998-1999*, London: Corporate Document Services.

Evandrou, M, Falkingham, J, Rake, K and Scott, A (2001) The dynamics of living arrangements in later life: evidence from the British Household Panel Survey, *Population Trends* 105: 37–44.

Glaser, K (1997) The living arrangements of elderly people, *Reviews in Clinical Gerontology* 7: 63–72.

Glaser, K and Grundy, E (1998) Migration and household change in the population aged 65 and over, 1971–1991, *International Journal of Population Geography* 4: 323–339.

Glaser, K, Hancock, R and Stuchbury, R (1998) *Attitudes in an Ageing Society* (Research sponsored by Age Concern England for the Millennium Debate of the Age), London: Age Concern Institute of Gerontology.

Glaser, K and Tomassini, C (2000) Proximity of older women to their children: a comparison of Britain and Italy, *The Gerontologist* 40: 729–737.

Grundy, E (1991) The demographic context of ageing, *The House Magazine* 16 (24 June): 19.

Grundy, E (1996) Population Review: (5) The population aged 60 and over, *Population Trends* 84: 14–20.

Grundy, E (1997) The health and health care of older adults in England and Wales, 1841–1994, in JC Charlton and M Murphy (eds) *The Health of Adult Britain* 1841–1994, vol. 2, London: The Stationery Office.

Grundy, E (1998) The epidemiology of aging, in R Tallis, H Fillit and JC Brocklehurst (eds) *Brocklehurst's Textbook of Geriatric Medicine and Gerontology*, 5th edn, London: Churchill Livingstone.

Grundy, E (1999) Intergenerational perspectives on family and household change in mid- and later life in England and Wales, in S McRae (ed.) *Changing Britain. Families and Households in the 1990s*, Oxford: Oxford University Press.

Grundy, E (2000) Co-residence of mid-life children with their elderly parents in England and Wales: changes between 1981 and 1991,

Population Studies 54: 193–206.

Grundy, E, Murphy, M and Shelton, N (1999) Looking beyond the household: intergenerational perspectives on living kin and contacts with kin in Great Britain, *Population Trends* 97: 19–27.

Hareven, TK (1992) Family and generational relations in the later years: a historical perspective, *Generations* 17: 7–12.

Haskey, J (1993) First marriage, divorce, and remarriage: birth cohort analyses, *Population Trends* 72: 24–33.

Jarvis, C (1993) *Family and friends in old age, and the implications for informal support: evidence from the British Social Attitudes Survey of 1986*, Working Paper No. 6, London: Age Concern Institute of Gerontology.

Keilman, N (1987) Recent trends in family and household composition in Europe, *European Journal of Population* 3: 297–325.

Kinsella, K and Velkoff, VA (2001) *An Ageing World: 2001*, Washington DC: US Government Printing Office.

Kobrin, FE (1976) The primary individual and the family: changes in living arrangements in the United States since 1940, *Journal of Marriage and the Family* 38: 233–239.

Kramarow, EA (1995) The elderly who live alone in the United States: historical perspectives on household change, *Demography* 32: 335–352.

Lilley, SJ, Brook, L, Park, A and Thomson, K (1997) *British Social Attitudes and Northern Ireland Social Attitudes 1995 Surveys, Technical Report*, London: SCPR.

Lin, G and Rogerson, PA (1995) Elderly parents and the geographic availability of their adult children, *Research on Aging* 17: 303–331.

Macunovich, DJ, Easterlin, RA, Schaeffer, CM and Crimmins, EM (1995) Echoes of the baby boom and bust: recent and prospective changes in living alone among elderly widows in the United States, *Demography* 32: 17–28.

Mancini, J and Bleiszner, R (1989) Aging parents and adult children, *Journal of Marriage and the Family* 51: 275–290.

McGarry, K and Schoeni, R (2000) Social security, economic growth, and the rise in the elderly widow's independence in the twentieth century, *Demography* 37: 221–236.

Mirrlees-Black, C, Mayhew, P and Percy, A (1996) *The 1996 British Crime Survey*, London: Home Office.

Murphy, M and Berrington, A (1993) Household change in the 1980s: a review, *Population Trends* 73: 18–26.

Murphy, M and Grundy, E (1994) Co-residence of generations and household structure in Britain: aspects of change in the 1980s, in H Becker and PLJ Hermkens (eds) *Solidarity of Generations: demographic, economic and social change, and its consequences*, vol. II, Amsterdam: Thesis Publishers.

Mutchler, JE (1992) Living arrangements and household transitions among the unmarried in later life, *Social Science Quarterly* 73: 565–580.

Ogawa, N and Retherford, RD (1997) Shifting costs of caring for the elderly back to families in Japan: will it work? *Population and Development Review* 23: 59–94.

ONS (1999) *Marriage, Divorce and Adoption Statistics, Series FM2 no. 24*, London: The Stationery Office.

Pampel, FC (1992) Trends in living alone among the elderly in Europe, in A Rogers (ed.) *Elderly Migration and Population Redistribution: a comparative study*, London: Belhaven Press.

Rogers, A (1988) Age patterns of elderly migration: an international comparison, *Demography* 25: 355–370.

Rowlands, O (1998) *Informal Carers*, London: The Stationery Office.

Ruddock, V, Wood, R and Quinn, M (1998) Birth statistics: recent trends in England and Wales, *Population Trends* 94: 12–18.

Shelton, N and Grundy, E (2000) Proximity of adult children to their parents in Great Britain, *International Journal of Population Geography* 6: 181–195.

Sundström, G (1994) Care by families: an overview of trends, in OECD (ed.) *Caring for Frail Elderly People. New Directions in Care*, vol. 14, Paris: OECD Social Policy Studies.

Taylor, MF, Brice, J, Buck, N and Prentice-Lane (eds) (2001) *British Household Panel Survey User Manual Volume A. Introduction, Technical Report and Appendices*, Colchester: University of Essex.

Tomassini, C and Wolf, D (2000) Stability and change in the living arrangements of older Italian women: 1990–1995, *Genus* LVI: 203–219.

UN (1999) *World Population Prospects: The 1998 Revision*, vol. I: Comprehensive Tables, New York: UN.

van Solinge, H (1994) Living arrangements of non-married elderly people in the Netherlands in 1990, *Ageing and Society* 14: 219–236.

Walker, A (1995) The family and the mixed economy of care – can they be integrated?, in I Allen and E Perkins (eds) *The Future of Family Care for Older People*, London: HMSO.

Wall, R (1995) Elderly persons and members of their households in England and Wales from preindustrial times to the present, in DI Kertzer and P Laslett (eds) *Aging in the Past*, Berkeley: University of California Press.

Warnes, A (1996) Migrations among older people, *Reviews in Clinical Gerontology* 6: 101–114.

Warnes, AM (1986) The residential mobility histories of parents and children, and relationships to present proximity and social integration, *Environment and Planning A* 18: 1581–1594.

Warnes, AM and Ford, R (1995) Housing aspirations and migration in later life: developments during the 1980s, *Papers in Regional Science: The Journal of the RSAI* 74: 361–387.

Wolf, DA (1994) The elderly and their kin: patterns of availability and access, in LG Martin and SH Preston (eds) *Demography of Aging*, vol. 29, Washington DC: Academy Press.

Wolf, DA (1995) Changes in the living arrangements of older women: an international study, *The Gerontologist* 35: 724–731.

COMMENTARY 1

Robin Darton

The information on household structure and the availability of informal support from spouses, children and, to a lesser extent, other kin links to the wider literature on informal care. A number of reasons for anticipating a decline in informal care have been suggested (Pickard *et al.* 2000):

- changes in the age structure of the population

- increases in the divorce rate

- a decline in family size

- increasing childlessness

- increasing employment rates among married women

- fewer older people living with their children

- changing care preferences

- changes in the nature of kinship obligations

The paper provides information on most of these developments. However, the question is not only whether we can continue to rely on informal care, but whether we should do so. In addition to the issue of informal care is the issue of choice of accommodation, and the relation between care in the home and care in alternative types of accommodation.

The paper takes the approach of looking at demographic trends, and this may be contrasted with a modelling approach, relating changes in the population to, for example, the demand for long term care.

Two approaches to the estimation of the likely level of informal care have been adopted: demand-led and supply-led. Both approaches have their weaknesses. Demand-led approaches have little meaning in practice in the absence of supply. Supply-led approaches ignore the relationship between informal care and the type of help needed, i.e. demand. Although informal help with practical or domestic tasks can come from a wide range of sources, informal help with personal or physical tasks usually comes from within the household. The dependency classification developed by Isaacs and Neville (1975) clearly corresponds to this. The authors' suggestion that 'nearby kin may be able to provide similar support to co-resident kin' needs to be qualified to refer to practical or domestic tasks. It should also be noted that caring for an older parent in a shared household is very stressful for carers.

The Personal Social Services Research Unit (PSSRU) has been developing a model to make projections to 2031 of likely demand for long term care services for people aged 65 and over, and the costs associated with meeting the expected demand (Wittenberg *et al.* 1998, 2001). The study informed the report of the Royal Commission on Long Term Care, and a more detailed study of informal care was also undertaken (Pickard *et al.* 2000). In this study, both demand and supply variables were included as predictors of informal care. The probability of receiving informal care was then simulated for future years, based on the analysis of the predictors of receipt of informal care in the present.

The analysis related to informal care for domestic tasks and employed the 1994/95 General Household Survey (GHS) 'elderly' data. Information about sources of help with personal care in the GHS was obtained only for those who could not perform the task without help, and thus the number of people for whom the information was available was small and incomplete. However, in addition to the receipt of informal care with domestic tasks, the model included household composition, which would also capture help with personal care tasks. A separate analysis of the small group who reported a source of help with personal care tasks (ninety-six individuals) showed that nearly 90 per cent obtained help from a spouse or other member of the household and only 4 per cent obtained informal help from outside the household. This is consistent with the results of larger studies.

Using the Government Actuary's Department (GAD) 1996-based marital status projections in the model suggested that the number of dependent older people living alone will increase by 45 per cent between 1996 and 2031, while the numbers living with others are projected to increase by 74 per cent. As a result, the proportion of dependent older people living alone was projected to fall from 43 per cent to 38 per cent.

These results differed from those based on the GAD's 1992-based projections, which had suggested that the number living alone would increase faster than the number living with others. Using these projections, the proportion of dependent older people living alone was projected to increase slightly, from 43 per cent to 44 per cent. However, the differences between the two sets of projections should not obscure the underlying trends. The revised projections still suggest that there will be a substantial rise in the numbers of dependent older people living alone, and those with personal care needs are unlikely to receive informal help with personal care to any great extent.

The projected rise in the number of married and cohabiting older people is greater in the 1996-based projections than in the 1992-based projections, and the difference is particularly marked for women. More older people, particularly older women, will have access to a spouse carer than previously anticipated. However, most spouse carers are also older people themselves, and may need support.

The model does not take into account changes in other relationships, in particular, informal care by children, a central concern of the paper under discussion. Changes in the supply of informal care have been explored by examining various scenarios allowing for changes in the supply of informal care or changes in policy towards carers. Alongside the decline in co-residence of older people with adult children, discussed in the paper, should be placed the evidence that older people are strongly opposed to moving in with a child if they become dependent and the stressful nature of this for carers, noted above. Using information from the GHS and assuming a decline in households formed by single dependent older people moving in with their children, indicates that more dependent older people will live alone and more will be admitted to institutions. However, the financial implications of this scenario were relatively close to the base case, mainly because the number of older people who are co-resident with their children is already very small.

Another scenario examined was that of increasing support for carers, making services more 'carer-blind'. This scenario also had relatively low cost implications, relative to the base case, since it was targeted on a particularly vulnerable group of co-resident carers; levels of service receipt among those living alone were low; and because it affected home care services, not institutional care.

For people entering residential and nursing home care without public funding, there is some evidence that lack of access to, or inadequate support from, informal carers and community services result in admissions at lower levels of dependency than for those receiving public funding (Netten and Darton 2001).

Other studies have suggested that informal care is likely to decline and that there will be an increase in living alone. The PSSRU model suggests that the numbers of people with informal help with domestic tasks will increase faster than those without. This is partly due to the differences between the 1992-based and the 1996-based GAD projections. In addition, the PSSRU model included legally married and cohabiting couples. The number of married couples is projected to fall, but the number of cohabiting couples is projected to rise at a faster rate. However, it is important to recognise that the treatment of cohabiting couples and married couples may not be the same.

Another analysis undertaken in the study has used the data from the 1998/99 GHS, which contained questions identifying people who needed regular daily help. The 1994/95 GHS was undertaken before the community care changes implemented in 1993 had become established. The analysis found evidence of high levels of targeting of services on people needing regular daily help; a marked increase in the use of private domestic help, compared with 1994/95; and a redistribution of formal services away from those with informal care (Pickard *et al.* 2001).

Concluding comments

- It is important to identify the care needs of all subgroups of the population, and to consider consequences of a change in status, e.g. from living with a spouse to becoming widowed. The treatment of people living as cohabiting couples is often unclear in analyses, they are likely to be an increasingly important group.

- It is important to monitor future trends. For example, current changes in the level of residential care and nursing home provision will have an impact on the PSSRU model.

- The types of care provided by informal carers need to be clarified. For example, non-resident kin cannot be expected to provide personal care, and older people may prefer professional care.

- Measures of housing satisfaction need to be linked to details of the environment. Improvements in housing standards may be one of the reasons for the preferences of an increasing majority to stay in their own home, but the environment may be unsuitable for frail older people, who then have little choice about alternatives.

- Analyses have often been based on rather small sample sizes, including the PSSRU model, and there is some concern about the reliability of the estimates. For the PSSRU model, the approach taken was to conduct sensitivity analyses. Some of the trends identified in the paper over the period 1991-1998 may not be statistically significant.

- Although the paper related to trends in Britain and Italy during the 1990s, the majority of the information related to Britain. International comparisons need to place demographic changes in the context of service patterns in order to provide useful lessons for other countries.

References

Isaacs, B and Neville, Y (1975) *The Measurement of Need in Old People*, Scottish Health Service Studies No. 34, Edinburgh: Scottish Home and Health Department.

Netten, A and Darton, R (2001) Formal and informal support prior to admission: are self-funders being admitted to care homes unnecessarily?, in S Tester, C Archibald, C Rowlings and S Turner (eds) *Quality in Later Life: rights, rhetoric and reality*. Proceedings of the British Society of Gerontology 30th Annual Conference, Stirling, 31 August–2 September 2001, Stirling, Scotland: Department of Applied Social Science, University of Stirling, pp. 60–64.

Pickard, L, Wittenberg, R, Comas-Herrera, A, Davies, B and Darton, R (2000) Relying on informal care in the new century? Informal care for elderly people in England to 2031, *Ageing and Society* 20(6): 745–772.

Pickard, L, Wittenberg, R, Comas-Herrera, A, Darton, R and Davies, B (2001) Community care for frail older people: analysis using the 1998/9 General Household Survey, in S Tester, C Archibald, C Rowlings and S Turner (eds) *Quality in Later Life: rights, rhetoric and reality*. Proceedings of the British Society of Gerontology 30th Annual Conference, Stirling, 31 August–2 September 2001, Stirling, Scotland: Department of Applied Social Science, University of Stirling, pp. 201–206.

Wittenberg, R, Pickard, L, Comas-Herrera, A, Davies, B and Darton, R (1998) *Demand for Long-Term Care: projections of long-term care finance for elderly people*, Personal Social Services Research Unit, University of Kent at Canterbury, London School of Economics and University of Manchester.

Wittenberg, R, Pickard, L, Comas-Herrera, A, Davies, B and Darton, R (2001) Demand for long-term care for older people in England to 2031, *Health Statistics Quarterly*, vol. 12, Winter 2001, London: The Stationery Office, pp. 5–17.

COMMENTARY 2
Vanessa Burholt

In discussing the paper by Karen Glaser and Cecilia Tomassini I will include some of the policy implications that have been raised by their findings. I shall give a Welsh slant to this discussion, as policy development in Wales is currently focusing on older people. At the time of writing (December 2001) the National Assembly for Wales are engaged in preparing a Strategy for Older People in Wales. One of the key themes in this document is housing services for older people. I will raise some of the issues that needed to be tackled in Wales, with relation to housing choices in later life.

In discussing the living arrangements of older people with regard to the receipt of care and proximity to family, and thinking about the implications for policy, it should be firmly acknowledged that a housing element cannot be dealt with in isolation (DETR 2000). The United Nations International Plan of Action on Ageing recommends that national housing policies should be concerned with:

> Co-ordinating policies on housing with those concerned with community services (social, health, cultural, leisure, communications) so as to secure, whenever possible, an especially favourable position for housing the aged vis-à-vis dwellings for the population at large.
>
> (UN/Division for Social Policy and Development 2000)

Housing has been described as the foundation of social care (National Housing Federation (NHF) 1999, Harrison and Heywood 2000) and is highlighted in the Framework for a National Housing Strategy for Wales (National Consultative

Forum on Housing in Wales 1999) as being an important factor in the success of 'community care', especially for older people wishing to remain in their own homes. However, most community care planning does not consider the housing needs of the majority of older clients living in their own homes (Harrison and Heywood 2000). The report *With Respect to Old Age* states that,

> Housing is another key element [for staying at home] and one which is neglected as a component of community care at national, local and individual level.
> (Royal Commission on Long Term Care 1999)

Despite the rhetoric that links should be established between health, social services and housing there is little evidence to suggest that strong relationships are developing (Royal Commission on Long Term Care 1999, Age Concern and RADAR 1999). For example, 45 per cent of local authorities in the UK do not operate joint teams between housing and social services or even work closely on the use of Disabled Facility Grants (Age Concern and RADAR 1999). It has been noted in *With Respect to Old Age* that housing is neglected in three realms: policy, practice and research (Royal Commission on Long Term Care 1999). *Quality and Choice: a decent home for all* (DETR 2000) states that local authorities need to co-ordinate resources and agencies that are required to deliver housing services.

It has been estimated that older people spend between 70 to 90 per cent of their time in their home (Baltes *et al.* 1990, 1993, Czaja 1988, Gabb *et al.* 1991, Hansen 1976). A majority of people aged 75 years and over prefer to remain autonomous in their own home for as long as possible, favouring the 'ageing in place' model (Butler and Lewis 1982, Filion *et al.* 1992, Lawton 1980, Lehr 1991, Oswald and Wahl 1995, Thomae 1988). The indications in Wales are that even very old people are highly motivated to retain mobility and independence and to remain in their own homes (Salvage 1986, Wenger *et al.* 1999). Throughout the 1980s and 1990s similar findings were shown elsewhere in the UK, that overwhelmingly older people desired to remain independent in their own homes (McCafferty 1994, Smith 1986, Tinker 1984, Warburton 1994). The United Nations International Plan of Action on Ageing states that:

> Adequate living accommodation and agreeable physical surroundings are necessary for the well-being of all people,

and it is generally accepted that housing has a great influence on the quality of life of any age group in any country. Suitable housing is even more important to the elderly, whose abodes are the centre of virtually all of their activities. Adaptations to the home, the provision of practical domestic aids to daily living and appropriately designed household equipment can make it easier for those elderly people whose mobility is restricted or who are otherwise disabled to continue to live in their own homes.

(UN/Division for Social Policy and Development 2000)

It is therefore crucial for policy to attend to the role of housing, living arrangements and receipt of help in the lives of older people.

Karen and Cecilia mentioned the changes in kin availability and have noted that other studies have suggested that: 'As the mothers of the "baby boom" generations age we may witness declines in the proportion of older women living alone, due to the increased availability of kin with whom they may co-reside.'

Even in light of increases in availability of kin I would suggest that there is not likely to be a significant increase in the proportion of older people co-residing with their children in the UK. The norms of society emphasise independence and we know that many older people are keen to keep their independence rather than burden their families with care duties (Moss and Moss 1992). These quotes are taken from the Bangor Longitudinal Study of Ageing (BLSA) and indicate typical reactions to moving in with children or other relatives:

Well I did think about [moving in with my sister]. But, it's all very well having a close relative handy but it's a different thing altogether to have to live with them day after day, and I did value my independence. She did too ... we kind of mutually agreed that it was a proposition which wasn't worth consideration.

Sometimes I get quivers and wonder what I'd do if I had to give up the house and I hate to think of it because I wouldn't like to be a burden on the children. They have their lives to live and they are just beginning now to be free of the responsibility of bringing their own children [up] and beginning to enjoy life together and I'd hate to go down and be a burden on them as an old person would be, you see.

(Burholt 1998)

The reticence on behalf of older people to burden their families has implications for the psychological wellbeing of both the older person and the carer. Karen and Cecilia have noted that: 'If the needs of frail older people cannot be met from within the household it is likely that these needs will be met by kin living in close proximity.'

However, family values regarding autonomy and independence play a critical role in determining the older person's reaction to help by adult children (Thomas 1988). Burholt and Wenger (2000) found that fewer parents felt emotionally very close to their children with the passage of time, although they had higher levels of contact and provision of help. The authors concluded that it was likely that dependency on instrumental help from children reduced emotional closeness. Other studies have found that intergenerational living arrangements are associated with lower subjective wellbeing, levels of satisfaction and greater levels of stress for older people and care-givers (Brackbill and Kitch 1991, Brody *et al.* 1978, Lawton *et al.* 1984, Mindel and Wright 1982).

A central theme invoked in discussions concerning the reliability of family support to older people is the role that modernisation has played in altering family structures and functions. In the study of intergenerational relationships, these discussions generally focus on three manifestations of modernisation:

1 economic development and geographic mobility;

2 urbanisation;

3 and the weakening of filial piety as a guiding principle of social life (Silverstein *et al.* 1998).

According to modernisation theory the more advanced the economy of a society, the lower the status accorded its older citizens (Cowgill 1986). This phenomenon is thought to operate as both education and occupation are targeted at younger people. In an economy characterised by rapid increases in knowledge and high levels of specialisation adult children are compelled to move away from their families of orientation in order to maximise their educational and occupational attainment (Silverstein *et al.* 1998). This mobility has resulted in greater geographic separation between the generations and a historical decline in the amount of contact between older parents and their adult children (Crimmins and Ingegneri 1990, Stearns 1989).

Indeed, adult children in most Western nations tend not to co-reside with their parents and often live far from them. This is taken by some as evidence that the intergenerational family is in decline and that older parents are isolated from their children in the modern family (Parsons 1944, Popenoe 1993, United Nations 1971). Differences in kinship structures appear to correlate with national economic development (Silverstein *et al.* 1998). For example, adult children in less developed southern and eastern European nations are more likely to live closer to their parents than are those in other European and North American nations (Hollinger and Haller 1990).

The degree of urbanisation is another manifestation of societal modernisation credited with fragmenting the intergenerational family through geographic separation. However, geographic dispersion of the generations appears to be mitigated by return migration of older people to their communities of origin, as poor health and the death of a spouse triggers the need for familial assistance (Feinstein and McFadden 1989, Lin and Rogerson 1995, Litwak and Longino 1987, Silverstein 1995).

Families are also guided by cultural beliefs or ideologies that guide which family forms are preferred and which are considered inappropriate. Variation in these beliefs are typically found between urban and rural sectors of society, and between more highly and less highly developed societies. In the United States, people raised in rural areas, especially on farms, express stronger filial responsibility than those raised in urban areas (Lee *et al.* 1994). The strong obligation toward elders in rural areas is thought to derive from the power that land ownership and control confers on older people (Nason 1981, Nydegger 1983, Salamon and Lockhart 1980, Tsuya and Martin 1992).

Although filial piety (unquestioned respect, responsibility, and sacrifice for family elders) is considered by some to be eroding as a central norm governing intergenerational relations in developing nations (Caffrey 1992, Cheung *et al.* 1994, Foner 1993), it is often characterised as having been completely lost in modern Western nations. Yet studies have consistently identified adult children as key sources of interaction and support for older parents in the most highly modernised societies, casting doubt on the conclusion that the contract between generations is truly abrogated (Duffy 1984, Hashimoto 1991, Johnson 1995). Although older parents in developed countries have less contact and are less likely to live with their children when compared with their counterparts in undeveloped and developing countries, neither do they appear to have been abandoned by their offspring (D'Costa 1985, Shanas 1973). In Western industrialised countries intergenerational solidarity – including intimacy, contact, the exchange of services – is maintained in spite of geographic separation (Litwak and Kulis 1987, Silverstein and Litwak 1993, Warnes 1994). This type of family (labelled the modified-extended family) has been heralded as an ideal intergenerational structure that meets the needs of dependent family members while serving the demand of a modern economy for a mobile labour force (Litwak 1985).

So we know that there are changing trends in the distance that older people live from their children, but we also know that older people don't necessarily want a family member to look after them. Where does this leave us in responding to the needs of older people with adequate policy measures?

Within Wales it is clear that we have to pay attention to the way that social care services are delivered to help maintain older people's independence in the community in whichever living arrangement they choose.

Firstly, this means that the new policy must pay attention to provision of small-scale services. Older people living at home consider housework services, washing net curtains, cleaning windows, gardening, decorating and handyperson services as essential in promoting successful independent living (Bartlett 1999, Clark *et al.* 1998, Heywood *et al.* 1999).

We also know that policy needs to include measures which will emphasise rehabilitation and supporting independence rather than focusing on responding to crisis. Preventive services are linked to enhanced rehabilitative services and are those which would prevent or delay the need for intensive domiciliary health or social care and would promote the quality of life of the older person by facilitating engagement in and with the community. Preventative schemes may include respite schemes for carers, telecare systems, energy efficiency projects and home security projects. For these schemes to be developed and delivered would require an inter-agency approach and pooling of funding. The Audit Commission (2000) notes that services for adults need re-engineering to meet future expectations. At present there is not an extensive or robust body of evidence to inform social care delivery, especially with regard to preventive services (Godfrey 1999).

The delivery of low level services and the provision of preventative services would address some of the features that Karen and Cecilia noted were most frequently cited by older people as being the one thing that they would like to improve about their homes, for example, the work load of the garden and the house, running costs of the house (in particular heating) and the risk of entry by burglars or intruders.

We know that we need to provide a care management system that is responsive to sudden changes as well as being sensitive to progressive deterioration (Moriarty and Webb 2000). We know that we need to provide services both to older people who live alone and those who live with carers, thereby reducing some of the strain that is currently felt by carers (Royal Commission on Long Term Care 1999). We also know that we need to ensure that older people are clear where and how they contact social services. They need to know what services they are entitled to and to be assured that they can complain about services without fear of having them removed (Audit Commission 2000, Carmel 1995, Hardy *et al*. 1999, Wilson 1995).

Secondly, as the current older population is replaced by the next cohort of retirees the housing preferences and living arrangements of this new group need to be assessed. It is likely that the attitudes of older people will change, with an increase in aspirations and expectations for choice and type of services (Cymdeithas Tai Eryri 1998). It has been noted that the National Assembly for Wales requires evidence to inform the housing strategy which is a 'robust assessment of housing need and demand across all tenures in Wales; reflective of local needs and priorities ... meeting the housing needs of future households' (National Consultative Forum on Housing in Wales 1999).

The availability of special forms of housing on the market that can meet the needs of older people may influence the choice to move or 'stay put'. There is evidence to suggest that the choice regarding type of housing may be more limited for renters than home owners (Bookbinder 1991) and that there is a lack of choice for tenants in the social sector (DETR 2000). In many areas of the United Kingdom the only form of social housing offered to older people is sheltered accommodation (Oldman and Greve 1983). The provision of this form of housing implicitly suggests that 'old age' is a problem, rather than a lack of affordable alternatives and adequate formal social care for those people who face declining functional abilities. I would argue that chronological age is not a good indicator of ability and therefore neither should it be used as a criterion for housing people in this form of adapted accommodation.

To date, much of the housing research in Wales has tended to be small scale, short term and only applicable to defined localities and new research is required to: identify social trends which would affect the housing market in order to develop a long-term view of housing policy; link housing with other areas of public policy in order to develop 'joined up thinking'; and to address issues in rural areas (National Assembly for Wales 1999). Research being conducted by Gwynedd Rural Ageing Network (GRAN) and the Institute of Medical and Social Care Research at the University of Wales, Bangor will address some of these issues, so crucial for future policy makers.

In April 2000 the National Assembly for Wales moved to address some of the longer term issues for older people presented by the lack of suitable housing. From 1 April 2001 all new *social housing* in Wales will be built to Lifetime Homes standards which meet the requirements of Part M of the building regulations (DETR 2000). This ruling should ensure that new houses are capable of adapting and meeting people's changing circumstances. Lifetime housing encompasses houses, flats and bungalows which are built to standards which allow flexibility, accessibility and adaptability, currently required to adhere to sixteen standards. These standards enable people with a range of disabilities to live more independently in the community (Belser and Weber 1995, Bonnet and Walliman 1996, Fisk and Hall 1997, Joseph Rowntree Foundation 1997, Raschko 1987), but are relatively inexpensive to include in new build (Cobbold 1997). The housing Green Paper, *Quality and Choice: a decent home for all* (DETR 2000) states that 'local housing strategies should include measures to promote improvement in the quality of all poor housing' across tenures. The Strategy for Older People in Wales now needs to consider whether to include a method of encouraging or enforcing private builders to incorporate these standards in new building. In addition, there needs to be incentives to encourage private landlords to upgrade buildings so that all tenures are accessible to all people regardless of age or functional abilities.

In conclusion, if social and economic changes continue to erode the neo-local basis for filial association, will the UK family be able to continue to adapt to new structural conditions or retract from providing care to its older members? Will the strength of normative prescriptions for family caregiving overcome the pull of urbanisation and migration? My expectation is that the family will be resilient to such social changes, as was apparent in the nineteenth century when a large out-migration of workers from rural areas did not result in the abandonment of older parents, due to the retention of select (mostly female) children (Patterson 1996). However, in order to marry the patterns of intergenerational solidarity to policy making, both researchers and policy makers need to be tuned in to the changes in older people's preferences for living arrangements, receipt of help, and housing. Only by attending to these preferences, can policy be developed that is able to respond to the needs of older people in society.

Acknowledgement

The section on the role that modernisation has played in altering family structures and functions relied heavily on the following paper: Silverstein, M, Burholt, V, Wenger, GC and Bengtson, VL (1998) Parent-child relations among very old parents in Wales and the United States: A test of modernization theory, *Journal of Aging Studies* 12(4): 387–409.

References

Age Concern and RADAR (1999) *Disabled Facilities Grants - Is the System Working?*, London: Age Concern and RADAR.

Audit Commission (2000) *Learning the Lessons from Joint Reviews of Social Services in Wales*, 1999/2000, Abingdon: Audit Commission Publications.

Baltes, MM, Wahl, H-W and Schmid-Furstoss, U (1990) The daily life of the elderly at home: activity patterns, personal control, and functional health, *Journal of Gerontology: Social Sciences* 45: 173–179.

Baltes, MM, Mayr, U, Borchelt, M, Maas, I and Wilms, H-U (1993) Everyday competence in old and very old age: an inter-disciplinary perspective, *Ageing and Society* 13(4): 657–580.

Bartlett, H (1999) Primary health care for older people: progress towards an integrated strategy?, *Health and Social Care in the Community* 7(5): 342–349.

Belser, SH and Weber, JA (1995) Home builders' attitudes and knowledge of aging: the relationship to design for independent living, in LA Pastalan (ed.) *Housing Decisions for the Elderly: to move or not to move*, New York: Haworth Press.

Bonnet, D and Walliman, N (1996) *Resident's Perceptions of Lifetime Homes*, London: David Bonnet Architects.

Bookbinder, D (1991) *Housing Options for Older People*, London: Age Concern.

Brackbill, Y and Kitch, D (1991) Intergenerational relationships: a social exchange perspective on joint living arrangements among the elderly and their relatives, *Journal of Aging Studies* 5(1): 77–97.

Brody, SJ, Poulshock W and Masciocchi, MA (1978) The family caring unit: a major consideration in the long-term support system, *The Gerontologist* 18(6): 556–561.

Burholt, V (1998) The Migration Process of Older People: the motivation for older people's residential relocation in rural North Wales,Working Paper, Centre for Social Policy Research and Development, Institute of Medical and Social Care Research, University of Wales, Bangor.

Burholt, V and Wenger, GC (1998) Differences over time in older people's relationships with children and siblings, *Ageing and Society* 18(5): 537–562.

Butler, RN and Lewis, MI (1982) *Aging and Mental Health: positive psychosocial and biomedical approaches*, 3rd edn, St Louis MS: C V Mosby.

Caffrey, RA (1992) Family care of the elderly in Northeast Thailand: changing patterns, *Journal of Cross Cultural Gerontology* 7: 105–116.

Carmel, S (1995) Satisfaction with hospitalisation: a comparative analysis of three types of services, *Social Science and Medicine* 21(11): 1243–9.

Cheung, CK, Lee, JJ and Chan, CM (1994) Explicating filial piety in relation to family cohesion, *Journal of Social Behavior and Personality* 9: 565–580.

Clark, H, Dyer, S and Horwood, J (1998) *That Bit of Help: the high value of low level preventative services for older people*, Bristol: Policy Press.

Cobbold, C (1997) *A Cost Benefit Analysis of Lifetime Homes*, York: Joseph Rowntree Foundation.

Cowgill, DO (1986) *Aging Around the World*, Belmont CA: Wadsworth.

Crimmins, E and Ingegneri, D (1990) Interaction and living arrangements of older parents and their children: past trends, present determinants, future implications, *Research on Aging* 12: 3–35.

Cymdeithas Tai Eryri (1998) *Gwynedd Care and Repair Review: consultative document*, Penygroes, Gwynedd: Care and Repair.

Czaja, S (1988) Safety and security of the elderly: implications for smart house design, *International Journal of Technology and Aging* 1(1): 49–67.

Department of the Environment, Transport and the Regions (2000)

Quality and Choice: a decent home for all, the Housing Green Paper. http://www.housing.detr.gov.uk/information/consult/homes/green/01.htm

D'Costa, R (1985) Family and generations in sociology: a review of recent research in France, *Journal of Comparative Family Studies* 16: 319–327.

Duffy, M (1984) Aging and the family: intergenerational psychodynamics, *Psychotherapy* 21: 342–346.

Feinstein, J and McFadden, D (1989) The dynamics of housing demand by the elderly: wealth, cash flow, and demographic effects, in DA Wise (ed.) *The Economics of Aging*, Chicago: University of Chicago Press.

Filion, P, Wister, A and Coblentz, EJ (1992) Subjective dimensions of environmental adaptation among the elderly: a challenge to models of housing policy, *Journal of Housing and the Elderly* 10(1/2): 3–32.

Fisk, M and Hall, D (1997) *Building Our Future: the housing challenge for Wales*, Cardiff: Institute of Welsh Affairs.

Foner, N (1993) When the contract fails: care for the elderly in nonindustrial cultures, in VL Bengtson and WA Achenbaum (eds) *The Changing Contract Across Generations*, Hawthorne NY: Aldine de Gruyter.

Gabb, B, Lodel, KA and Combs, ER (1991) User input in housing design: the interdisciplinary challenge, *Home Economics Research Journal* 20: 16–25.

Godfrey, M (1999) *Preventive Strategies for Older People: mapping the literature on effectiveness and outcomes*, Kidlington: Anchor Trust.

Hansen, GD (1976) Meeting housing challenges: involvement-the elderly, *Housing Issues. Proceedings of the Fifth Annual Meeting, American Association of Housing Educators*, Lincoln NE: University of Nebraska Press.

Hardy, B, Young, R and Wistow, G (1999) Dimensions of choice in the assessment and care management process: the views of older people, carers and care managers, *Health and Social Care in the Community* 7(6): 483–491.

Harrison, L and Heywood, F (2000) *Health Begins at Home: planning at the health-housing interface for older people*, Bristol: Policy Press.

Hashimoto, A (1991) Living arrangements of the aged in seven developing countries: a preliminary analysis, *Journal of Cross Cultural Gerontology* 6: 359–381.

Heywood, F, Pate, A, Means, R and Galvin J (1999) *Housing Options for Older People (HOOP): report on a developmental project to refine a housing option appraisal tool for use by older people*, London: Elderly Accommodation Counsel.

Hollinger, F and Haller, M (1990) Kinship and social networks in modern societies: a cross-cultural comparison among seven nations, *European Sociological Review* 6: 103–124.

Johnson, CL (1995) The parent-child relationship in late life. Paper presented at the Annual Conference of the American Gerontological Association in Los Angeles, CA.

Joseph Rowntree Foundation (1997) *Building Lifetime Homes*, York: Joseph Rowntree Foundation.

Lawton, MP (1980) *Environment and Aging*, Monterey CA: Brooks/Cole.

Lawton, MP, Moss, MS and Kleban, MH (1984) Marital status, living arrangements, and the well-being of older people, *Research on Aging* 6(3): 323–345.

Lee, GR, Coward, RT and Netzer, JK (1994) Residential differences in filial responsibility expectations among older persons, *Rural Sociology* 59: 100–109.

Lehr, U (1991) *Pschologie des Alterns*, 7th edn, (Psychology of Aging), Heidelberg, Wiesbaden: Quelle and Meyer.

Lin, G and Rogerson, PA (1995) Elderly parents and the geographic availability of their adult children, *Research on Aging* 17: 303–331.

Litwak, E (1985) *Helping the Elderly: the complementary roles of informal networks and formal systems*, New York: Guilford Press.

Litwak, E and Kulis, S (1987) Technology, proximity, and measures of kin support, *Journal of Marriage and the Family* 49: 649–661.

Litwak, E and Longino, CF (1987) Migration patterns among the elderly: a developmental perspective, *The Gerontologist* 27: 266–272.

McCafferty, P (1994) *Living Independently: a study of housing needs of elderly and disabled people*, London: HMSO.

Mindel, CH and Wright, R (1982) Satisfaction in multigenerational households, *Journal of Gerontology* 37(4): 483–489.

Moriarty, J and Webb, S (2000) *Part of Their Lives: community care for older people with dementia*, Bristol: Policy Press.

Moss, MS and Moss, SZ (1992) Themes in parent-child relationships when elderly parents move nearby, *Journal of Aging Studies* 6(3): 259–271.

Nason, J (1981) Respected elder or old person: aging in a Micronesian community, in P Amoss and S Harell (eds) *Other Ways of Growing Old*, Stanford CA: Stanford University Press.

National Assembly for Wales (1999) *A Housing Research Audit for Wales*, Cardiff: The National Assembly for Wales.

National Consultative Forum on Housing in Wales (1999) *A Framework for a National Housing Strategy for Wales*, Cardiff: National Assembly for Wales.

National Housing Federation (1999) *Housing for Health*, London: National Housing Federation.

Nydegger, CN (1983) Family ties of the aged in cross-cultural perspective, *The Gerontologist* 23: 26–32.

Oldman, C and Greve, J (1983) *Sheltered Housing for the Elderly: policy, practice and the consumer*, London: George Allen and Unwin.

Oswald, F and Wahl, HW (1995) On the individual meaning of home: an empirical study with healthy and mobility impaired elderly. Paper presented at the 48th Annual Scientific Meeting of the Gerontological Society of America, Los Angeles, CA.

Parsons, T (1944) The social structure of the family, in R N Anshen (ed.) *The Family: its function and destiny*, New York: Harper.

Patterson, N (1996) Conflicting norms in modern British kinship: case studies of domestic violence and competition for care in North Wales, circa 1920–1996. Working paper, Centre for Social Policy Research and Development, University of Wales, Bangor.

Popenoe, D (1993) American family decline, 1960-1990: a review and appraisal, *Journal of Marriage and the Family* 55: 527–555.

Raschko, B (1987) Universal design, *ASID Report* 13(2): 8–10.

Royal Commission on Long Term Care (1999) *With Respect to Old Age: long term care – rights and responsibilities. Alternative model of care for older people*, vol. 2, London: The Stationery Office.

Salamon, S and Lockhart, V (1980) Land ownership and the position of elderly in farm families, *Human Organization* 39: 324–331.

Salvage, A (1986) *Attitudes of the Over 75s to Health and Social Services*, Cardiff: University College of Wales.

Shanas, E (1973) Family-kin networks and aging in cross-cultural perspective, *Journal of Marriage and the Family* 35: 505–511.

Silverstein, M (1995) Stability and change in temporal distance between the elderly and their children, *Demography* 32: 29–45.

Silverstein, M, Burholt, V, Wenger, GC and Bengtson, VL (1998) Parent-child relations among very old parents in Wales and the United States: a test of modernization theory, *Journal of Aging Studies* 12(4): 387–409.

Silverstein, M and Litwak, E (1993) A task-specific typology of intergenerational family structure in later life, *The Gerontologist* 33: 258–264.

Smith, K (1986) *I'm Not Complaining*, London: Shelter Housing Advice Centre.

Stearns, PN (1989) Historical trends in intergenerational contacts, *Journal of Children in Contemporary Society* 20: 21–32.

Thomae, H (1988) *Das Individuum und seine Welt (2, völlig neu bearbeitete Auflage.)* (The individual and its world, 2nd edn), Göttingen: Hogrefe.

Thomas, JL (1988) Predictors of satisfaction with children's help for younger and older elderly parents, *Journals of Gerontology* 43(1): S9–S14.

Tinker, A (1984) *Staying at Home: helping elderly people to stay at home*, London: HMSO.

Tsuya, N and Martin, L (1992) Living arrangements of elderly Japanese and attitudes toward inheritance, *Journals of Gerontology* 47: S45–S54.

United Nations (1971) *Question of the Elderly and the Aged*, General Assembly, A/8364, 31 August, New York: United Nations.

United Nations/Division for Social Policy and Development (2000) *The United Nations International Plan of Action on Ageing*, New York: United Nations.

Warburton, W (1994) *Home and Away: a review of recent evidence to explain why some older people enter residential care while others stay at home*, London: Department of Health.

Warnes, AM (1994) Residential mobility through the life course and proximity of family members to elderly people, in UN Department of Economic and Social Information and Policy Analysis, *Ageing and the Family*, New York: United Nations.

Wenger, GC, Burholt, V and Scott, A (1999) *Final Report to NHS Wales Office of Research and Development: Bangor Longitudinal Study of Ageing 1994–1999*, Centre for Social Policy Research and Development, Institute of Medical and Social Care Research, University of Wales, Bangor.

Wilson, G (1995) Low expectations reinforced: experiences of health services in advanced old age, in G Wilson (ed.) *Community Care: asking the user*, London: Chapman and Hall.

5 The relationship between current policies on long term care and the expectations of older people

Isobel Allen

I have recently been archiving thirty years of research and it has taken me rather a long time. One of the reasons, of course, is that I have found myself reading, not only the research and reports for which I was personally responsible, but also the myriad of literature, articles, census reports and other documents which I unaccountably collected over the years.

As I came to write this paper, I realised that within the files and boxes that most people would have thrown away years ago, there was a treasure trove of information on the development of health and social policy in the latter part of the twentieth century. What I would like to examine in this paper is how, and on what basis, policy towards older people developed over those years. I will challenge some of the received assumptions about what older people actually want and I will argue that many of these assumptions have been based somewhat more on what has suited policy makers rather than a rigorous investigation of the views of people themselves.

Residential care and choice

I would like to go back some years in looking at what has been happening to residential care for older people. Peter Townsend really took it apart in *The Last Refuge* (Townsend 1962) – and I think that the title of that book had an enormous influence on the subsequent thinking about residential care – both for good and perhaps for ill. It was clear that the concept of the 'workhouse' was still prevalent at the time of the study, in 1959, and one of the most important findings was that an astonishing 88 per cent of residents of local authority homes were sleeping in rooms of three or more beds in 1959. These were hardly places where independence and privacy were valued. Perhaps it was not surprising that a consensus started to emerge that older people should stay in their own homes for as long as possible and that residential care was actually the last resort, rather than the last refuge.

So the move towards community care started in the 1960s, with the commendable desire to move people out of huge institutions – not only residential homes but also the long-stay psychiatric and general hospitals. It is perhaps not surprising that successive governments have shown a great interest in the concept of 'community care', most particularly since the early 1980s. It was not purely altruistic, of course, since originally it was thought to be cheaper for people to live in the community rather than in institutions funded by the state. One of the main reasons for this was because much of the care in the community could be given by family members or 'carers' as we learnt to call them.

It was interesting to see how the desire to save public funds became entwined with the received wisdom that people should stay in the community as long as possible. To quote from the 1981 White Paper *Growing Older* (DHSS 1981a), since it shows how a concept can become immortalised as 'a good thing', without a proper critical assessment being made of the full implications of what it means – for everyone concerned:

> Whatever level of public expenditure proves practicable, and however it is distributed, the primary sources of support and care for elderly people are informal and voluntary. These spring from the personal ties of kinship, friendship and neighbourhood. They are irreplaceable. It is the role of public authorities to sustain, and where necessary, develop – but never to displace – such support and care. Care in the community must increasingly mean care by the community.

This rather flowery evocation of a caring community was followed by a Department of Health and Social Security *Report of a Study of Community Care* (DHSS 1981b), which recognised that 'the strength of informal support available to people is often critical to the feasibility and cost-effectiveness of community based packages of care ... all depend for their success on a high level of commitment from informal carers.' This was a nod in the direction of carers, and perhaps a recognition that their contribution was not as cost-free as the White Paper had implied. And was this the first sighting of the phrase which came to dominate the agenda – 'packages of care'?

So increased care in the community was government policy in the 1980s but, at the same time, that government was particularly interested in the development of the private and voluntary sector in the delivery of social services. Norman Fowler's (the then secretary of state for social services) seminal speech at the annual social services conference in Buxton in 1984 called for social services departments to become 'enabling' authorities – moving away from delivering services themselves to commissioning and purchasing services from the independent sector.

Interestingly, the move towards the private sector was already afoot, through changes elsewhere in government. This had led to a huge increase in the numbers of older people entering private residential care in the early 1980s, with a high proportion funded by the social security budget without any assessment of need, unlike those entering local authority homes. The Audit Commission in *Making a Reality of Community Care* identified this as a 'perverse incentive' towards institutional care (Audit Commission 1986). The Griffiths Report of 1988 followed this up by recommending a more co-ordinated approach to the funding and management of care, with social services departments taking the responsibility for the allocation of funds, the assessment of need and the co-ordination of care (Griffiths 1988). And then came the 1989 White Paper *Caring for People* (DHSS 1989) and the NHS and Community Care Act of 1990 which largely adopted the recommendations of the Griffiths Report.

It was quite clear that certain policies had been pulling against one another. On the one hand the encouragement of the private sector was being fuelled by the financial incentives from the social security budget. But on the other hand, not only had this led to an explosion in the social security budget but it also encouraged residential care at the expense of community care. In addition, there was a paradox in that older people were said to want to stay at home as long as possible and yet, given access to public funds without assessment, appeared to have been flocking into private residential homes at an unprecedented rate. There was some dispute about whether they were going of their own accord, or whether they were being pushed by carers who were not quite as willing to take on the caring responsibility as government papers suggested they ought to be. But I think it is fairly clear that many of them were grasping with both hands the opportunity to be looked after, and that many of them were exercising what came to be called 'a positive choice'. This opportunity was not to last for long however.

There is general agreement that the immediate consequence of the NHS and Community Care Act, which came into force in April 1993, was that fewer people entered residential care and more received care in the community. Therefore it appeared that the choice of most people to stay at home had increased. However, there was little or no discussion about whether choice had been denied to those who had wanted to enter residential care but had not been assessed as being in need of it, and whether those who were staying at home were getting much choice in the services they received.

Choice and community care

The key components of community care, spelt out in *Caring for People*, were (i) services that respond flexibly and sensitively to the needs of individuals and their carers; (ii) services that allow a range of options for consumers; (iii) services that intervene no more than is necessary to foster independence; and (iv) services that concentrate on those with the greatest needs. At the heart of the government's policy at the time were two statements in *Caring for People*: 'Promoting choice and independence underlies all the Government's proposals' and 'Community care means providing the right level of intervention and support to enable people to achieve maximum independence and control over their lives.'

Increasing choice for users and carers has been one of the cornerstones of government policy over the last decade. One of the key aims both of the White Paper *Caring for People* and the NHS and Community Care Act was to ensure that older people had increased opportunities to stay at home rather than enter residential care. It was agreed that this was the choice of most older people and that more resources should be put into enabling them to satisfy that choice. In addition, much stress was put on the need for 'packages of care' to be put together, using the needs of older people and their carers as the point of departure rather than presenting them with available services. The move from a 'service-led' system of assessment to a 'needs-led' system was central to the new approach to ensuring choice for users and carers.

It has always been clear that the concept of choice is not easy to reconcile with the reality of the availability of resources. The implication of promoting choice and independence for users and carers is that there is a range of services potentially available to them, from which they can pick those which satisfy their needs. The reality is that this is simply not feasible, since the demand would clearly soon outstrip the supply. Resources are not unlimited, so a rationing procedure has to be brought into play. The composition of a package of care has to be made by assessment of need against a background of equitable distribution of limited resources. It is the assessment of need which therefore effectively rations the services available. A 'needs-led' assessment may listen to the users' and carers' needs, but the nature and intensity of the services in the package of care supplied are still constrained by what resources are available to meet the overall demand. If the resources are not increased, in fact, the rationing result remains the same as when the process was service-led, but perhaps it allows policy makers and providers to feel better about it.

In *Elderly People: Choice, Participation and Satisfaction* (Allen *et al.* 1992), we looked at some of the issues surrounding 'choice' and pointed out that it might be misleading to use the language of the market-place in discussing health and social care services. The implication of increased choice is that, given the information, users of services will be able to select the 'best buy' from a range of possibilities, all of which are available to them. They should be able to stipulate what they want, when they want it, how they want it mixed with other services, who will deliver it and how much they will receive.

In fact, of course, few, if any, older people are able to operate in such a way. Most of those we interviewed had no choice of what went into their package of services, the time at which the service was delivered, the person who delivered it or how much they received. The 'mix' of services was very limited, and most people only had one or two services in the packages, with not much of either. We concluded that there was an urgent need for an examination of the apparent contradiction between the emphasis on consumer choice and the reality of a resource-constrained supply of care, with access to it controlled by 'assessment' and continuing participation in it controlled by 'care management'.

A few years later Ruth Young and colleagues from the Nuffield Institute for Health found that while care managers supported the shift towards a needs-led approach, users and carers perceived the processes in a different way and found the system complex and confusing (Young *et al.* 1999). Real choice was clearly constrained and users and carers still felt they had little sense of control over the decision-making process concerning which of their needs were to be met, and how. Most of them felt powerless and even those who had begun to get the measure of the system were still highly dependent on care managers to agree additional services, change the provider organisation or alter elements of the care package. It is not clear that much had changed since our study, and one has to question whether it has since the Nuffield Institute study conducted in the late 1990s.

In the PSI study we also warned against the increased targeting of resources, with people in the greatest need being given more and more intensive packages of care, while people not assessed as being in such need receiving little or nothing at all. We argued that more preventative services for more people might perhaps be of greater value in keeping older people out of residential care than concentrating services on a very few. We noted at the time: 'This may not be a fashionable view, but our findings indicate that much closer attention should be paid to it.' Since that time there has been the introduction of the Prevention Grant and Partnership Special Grants (1999) – now known as the Promoting Independence Grants. This has undoubtedly been successful in many areas, but the extent to which it is sufficient, and how it is actually used, are points for discussion.

The language in recent policy statements has not changed much in the last few years. 'Needs-led' assessments and care management are now enshrined as quality measures (Department of Health/SSI 2001). Promoting independence is the key concept now, although I still find that a bit hard to apply to many of the older people I have interviewed over the years. I suppose it depends what is meant by independence.

The key concept of the 1989 White Paper *Caring for People* was 'Promoting *choice* and independence'. What has happened to choice? Has it been dropped? There is certainly an emphasis today, which was not there even five years ago, on 'intensive prevention of avoidable admission to hospital or a residential or nursing home'. The phrase 'avoidable admission' resonates well with the policy as it has developed over the past thirty years, but I would question where the concept of choice has gone within that phrase. Whose choice are we looking at? The emphasis on intensive prevention appears to have led to a decrease in admissions to residential or nursing care, but I wonder at what cost – both to older people and their carers who are receiving this intensive care, and to those people who are no longer able to receive the semi-intensive care that might keep them out of residential care – and so on down the ladder of need.

Recent trends

What has happened in recent years? Just looking at the home care and home help figures (Department of Health 2001a), we can see that the number of 'contact hours' has increased by 12 per cent between 1996 and 2000, while the number of households receiving home care decreased by 23 per cent. Home help carers are spending more time with fewer clients – the average number of contact hours per household increased by 45 per cent between 1996 and 2000. All the indications are that this trend is accelerating. There is also clear evidence that the contribution of the independent sector in home care provision has been increasing at a steady rate and that it now provides more hours than local authorities (Department of Health 2001b).

At the same time, the number of people over 65 supported by local authorities in residential and nursing homes increased by 7 per cent over the same period, but it is perhaps more interesting that there was a decrease in numbers between 2000 and 2001 (Department of Health 2001c). So, in fact, there has actually been a decrease in the numbers receiving packages of care *and* a decrease in the numbers in residential care. The numbers of those receiving *intensive* home care have actually gone up – those receiving more than ten contact hours and six or more visits a week – but, of course, this appears to be at the expense of those receiving less intensive packages. One of the things that is of most concern in all this is that these are all part of a whole battery of performance measures. Local authorities are being judged in terms of 'performing well or badly' on these indicators, but I must confess to feeling rather uneasy about the reality behind these figures and the basis on which these value judgements are being made.

What has been happening in assessment of need? How frail do you need to be to be assessed as needing community or residential care? If you do a bit of arithmetic on the figures you find that the average household received 6.7 hours of home care a week in 2000. This was a considerable increase on the type of packages we found in our 1992 study (Allen *et al*. 1992). Resources were certainly being concentrated on those most in need, it appeared. But looking at that a bit more coldly, it still only amounted to less than an hour a day on average, even if it was supplemented by other community care services, such as meals, day care and so on. Even the ten hours a week minimum of an intensive care package only amounts to less than two hours a day.

What kind of package will the local authority pay for before you are deemed as needing residential care? Figures are hard to come by and there are wide regional differences but it looks as though a London local authority will find it difficult to fund a package which requires more than three hours of care a day – at a cost of around £250 a week if it is a simple package.

It is here that the question arises of whether even three hours of care a day is enough for people who need a lot of care. There must certainly be an assumption in this kind of package that other people will be providing care as well, if an older person is very frail. But who is asking older people and their carers if this is really what they want? Are they really so much against residential care – or is the whole policy based on a misunderstanding of what people are saying?

Hearing the voice of the consumer

I have always been interested in listening to what people actually say, when you get behind the large-scale surveys and the satisfaction ratings and the battery of other standard measurements. In this part of the paper I would like to look at some of the results from my own studies and more recent investigations in residential care. The picture of everyone clinging at all costs to their independence and autonomy in their own homes is, I think, rather misleading and not in fact based on hard evidence.

What do people actually think of residential care? First of all, and most importantly I think, many of those we interviewed were pleasantly surprised at what they found when they entered a home. In our study, 60 per cent said that it was much better than they thought it was going to be – and so did their carers. I think that this underlines the fact that image-building for residential care is needed. It is clearly difficult to get over the message that residential care might be a positive choice. We certainly found that the social workers we interviewed at the time were often presenting residential care as a last resort. I suspect this may still be so.

In many instances we came across an enormous sense of relief among older people in the homes – of safety, of being looked after, of not being an endless source of worry to their carers, of getting regular meals, of not worrying about heating, cleaning, shopping, bills and so on. These findings were echoed in recent work conducted by Gillian Dalley and Sarah Hadley in Camden (Dalley and Hadley 2000) and Leonie Kellaher in Methodist homes (Kellaher 2000). Back in the 1980s, I remember lots of discussion among professionals about older people needing to maintain their independence, and endless discussions about providing tea and coffee-making facilities and little kitchens to make snacks. What we saw when we went round the homes was a lot of these facilities gathering dust and older people looking forward to being waited on by someone bringing them tea. They had been making tea all their lives – and now someone else was doing it. So what of promoting independence?

Above all – in all the studies in which I have been involved, I have noted how much the older people liked the food – the variety, the choice, the quantity. As one woman who had lived alone said: '*I like the food. It's beautiful. It's like Christmas every day.*'

Do older people want a choice of mealtimes – as so many experts asserted in the 1980s? I am not so sure. I have carried out many an interview when, as 12 o'clock approached, people would start looking at their watches and listening for the sound of footsteps making for the dining room: '*I hope this isn't going to take much longer – I can't miss my lunch.*'

Older people liked the staff, and were often fulsome in their praise: '*You get looked after. It's the first rest I've had for years. It's care, attention and kindness.*' Both Gillian Dalley and Leonie Kellaher found the same thing in 2000. Two of Kellaher's respondents pointed to the benefits of residential care for them. One described herself as a loner, but added: '*My way of life has improved. I hated cooking and laundry. I'm very happy here. I'm fulfilled. I enjoy every minute of the day.*' And the other pointed to the additional freedom gained from having things done for her: '*You are waited on, meals got for you and there is no shopping.*'

Of course, not everything in residential care is so rosy – and most studies will show the downside – often related to the other residents who were sometimes found very irritating or unsettling, particularly if they were mentally frail. In addition, residents usually find it difficult to complain, and we found in our study that people were anxious about complaining and thought if they did they would be regarded as nuisances or worse. But we found that this was also true of those receiving community care, and we concluded that this was one of the main reasons why older people could rarely be regarded as active consumers able to exercise choice and independence. So many of these words can become meaningless slogans when applied to people who are very old and frail, and people in residential care today are very old and often very frail.

You invariably do not get into a residential home, certainly with local authority funding, unless you are both. In 1995, according to a PSSRU survey the average age on admission to residential care homes of all types was 83.5 and to nursing homes was 82.5 (Netten *et al.* 2001). Back in 1981, according to an earlier PSSRU survey, the average age on admission was 79 for local authority homes, 77.8 for voluntary homes and 81.7 for private homes (PSSRU 1981).

The 1995 PSSRU survey found that around 40 per cent of all those admitted to residential and nursing homes were suffering from some form of diagnosed dementia, and it was noted that nearly a third of those who were identified as having severe cognitive impairment had not officially been diagnosed. There was, in fact, evidence of widespread cognitive impairment among people admitted to care homes.

The analysis revealed five factors which were associated with increased probabilities of placement in residential care: arthritis, deafness, family breakdown, living alone and lack of motivation. The authors make an interesting comment on 'lack of motivation' by saying that 'high levels of functional impairment may be partly the result of lack of motivation, suggesting that this may be an appropriate target group for rehabilitation services as an alternative to admission to long-term care.'

I wonder if this is really the correct interpretation of the data. Is it not possible that lack of motivation may be the result of 'high levels of functional impairment' rather than the other way round? Is it not possible that some people simply run out of puff, particularly in their mid-eighties, and that they actually would like to be looked after and brought their tea, rather than having a rehabilitation programme?

Conclusions

I would like to return to the question of whether the constant emphasis in recent years on the benefits of care in the community has not detracted from the possibility that residential care might, in some cases, be a preferable option to living in increasingly difficult circumstances in the community. In all my studies, and in more recent studies, there has been evidence of a strong measure of relief among many older people who had found residential care much more attractive than they had expected, valuing the care, the security and the company it offered. Many of them were old and tired and happy to be looked after, having lived on their own for many years. For them the decision to enter residential care might not have been a 'positive' choice, but it was not a negative one either. For many it had turned out to be a positive solution.

And this is also true of many carers. The discussion about carers has been rather muted recently. They were certainly the flavour of the 1990s as their needs were recognised and much was made of their contribution. But their choices are important too, and there can be little doubt that the burden on them today is just as great – if not greater – as it was in the studies conducted in the 1980s and 1990s. These packages of care with an average of less than seven hours a week are hardly likely to make a lot of difference to people caring for very dependent older people, and even packages of three hours a day are often not supplied to people with carers. Perhaps carers would also welcome a 'positive choice'.

There is a danger that the value of residential care for older people will be overlooked in the current drive towards promoting independence through staying in the community. If the concept of choice is to be maintained, there should be a recognition that there must be sufficient capacity and resources available to ensure that residential care continues to be an available option, not only for those who meet increasingly stringent eligibility criteria, but also for those who would welcome the security, comfort and care offered by good residential care homes.

References

Allen, I, Hogg, D and Peace, S (1992) *Elderly People: choice, participation and satisfaction*, London: Policy Studies Institute.

Audit Commission (1986) *Making a Reality of Community Care*, London: HMSO.

Dalley, G and Hadley, S (2000) *Best Value? The Report of a Study of the Views of Users of Camden Council's Services for Older People*, London: Centre for Policy on Ageing.

Department of Health and Social Security (1981) *Growing Older*, Cm. 8173, London: HMSO.

Department of Health and Social Security (1981) *Report of a Study of Community Care*, London: HMSO.

Department of Health and Department of Social Security (1989) *Caring for People: community care in the next decade and beyond*, Cm. 849, London: HMSO.

Department of Health/Social Services Inspectorate (2001) *Improving Older People's Services: inspection of social care services for older people*, London: Department of Health.

Department of Health (2001a) *Adults: home help and home care trends (all sectors)*, Personal Social Services Statistics, Table C6, London: Department of Health.

Department of Health (2001b) *Adults: contact hours of home help and home care provided, by sector*, Personal Social Services Statistics, Table C5, London: Department of Health.

Department of Health (2001c) *Adults: local authority supported residents in staffed residential and nursing care at 31 March*, Personal Social Services Statistics, Table C7, London: Department of Health.

Griffiths, R (1988) *Community Care: an Agenda for Action*, London: HMSO.

Kellaher, L (2000) *A Choice Well Made: mutuality as a governing principle in residential care*, London: Centre for Policy on Ageing and Methodist Homes.

Netten, A, Darton, R, Bebbington, A and Brown, P (2001) Residential or nursing home care? The appropriateness of placement decisions, *Ageing and Society* 21: 3–23.

Personal Social Services Research Unit (1981) *Survey of Residential Accommodation of the Elderly*, 1981, Discussion Paper 277, University of Kent.

Townsend, P (1962) *The Last Refuge*, London: Routledge and Kegan Paul.

Young, R, Hardy, B and Wistow, G (1999) *Whose Choice? How users, carers and care managers see the assessment and care management system*, Evidence Briefing Paper 4, Personal Social Services Unit, London School of Economics and Nuffield Institute for Health University of Leeds.

COMMENTARY 1
Helena Herklots

Isobel Allen's paper has opened the debate about what the policies on long term care are doing in terms of constraining people's choices or enabling those choices. There are some major problems with policies on long term care. Firstly, they are not consistent with each other or with other aspects of government policy. More importantly, as suggested in Isobel's paper, they do not actually reflect the needs and wants of the older population. In considering the reasons for that most people would immediately think of cost as a constraint on delivering what people want, and we certainly heard that in relation to community care. I think it is actually much more than that. We need a debate about how the cake is divided. There is also a debate about the size of the cake. Under the previous Conservative governments, we were perhaps very pessimistic about the options for actually talking about the size of the budget. We have moved on somewhat and we can now start doing that. It is also about such things as political will or political beliefs, and about the different myths that grow up about different forms of care, which is very much what Isobel was highlighting: that, 'truths' become imbedded in the system, and it is these that are almost more damaging than anything else.

An example of this is when very complex policies get translated into what can be called 'policy images', such as 'selling homes to pay for care'. The whole long term care debate appeared to come down to that one phrase. So public policy has tried to deal with the issue of selling your home to pay for care, rather than a whole host of issues that long term care is concerned with. We have a tangled web of policies in this area. One of these is about the payment arrangements. If a person does need to move into a care home, they no longer have to sell their house if the local authority offers them the deferred 'payment option'. The house will eventually be sold to pay the bill, but after the person has died. Politically, it has answered the problem but it has done very little for the actual complexity of long term care issues. So what are some other of these policy images to which I have referred? Well one that Isobel raised in her paper was the 'last refuge', or the 'last resort'.

There is the myth that residential and nursing care is always the last resort for people. So we hear 'don't put me in a home', and it creates a strong negative image. What does that do to the thousands of people who work in care homes? What about the quality of life people would expect if they moved into a care home? How does that influence the debate about funding levels for care? We know, as a fact, that funding levels for older people in residential care are lower than for younger people. The other image that we have is that older people always want to stay in their own homes which is, again, a point Isobel raised. What has happened, of course, is that the professionals and the policy makers have given a very narrow definition of what community care is all about, as if it is actually about an hour of support in your home a day. I think we are in real danger of institutionalising people in their own homes. If you think about what defines an institution – things like lack of stimulation and lack of control – if you are struggling in your own home, and you have your allocation of two half-hour visits, to some degree I believe you are at risk of institutionalisation. Another policy issue is that of traditional sheltered housing being widely regarded as yesterday's product; that many such schemes are simply not wanted any more by older people. The idea that we need to move on and find something new and exciting – we can do much better.

It is of course much more complex than that. Yes, some sheltered housing is hard to let and some is not, and some is still very popular. There is very little new development in sheltered housing. But we have a legacy in the UK of sheltered housing and we need to think about what change of approaches and thinking we could bring to that. Finally, I think we are in danger of creating another sort of policy myth, which is that extra care housing is the answer – the new solution. It provides care, enables one to maintain 'independence', and if only we developed more extra care housing schemes, we would solve the problem, or would we? One of the issues with extra care is that it tends to be defined in relation to other forms of care, as if it is a better form of housing and support than residential care, and offers more than sheltered housing, rather than people thinking about what it is in itself. It very much responds to the current funding and regulatory framework, it has a niche within this framework; this may not be so in the future. However, it is popular and undoubtedly for some older people it is a very positive option.

So these are some of the sorts of myths and images that affect the way in which policy is actually developed. Should we move away from that and look at what older people want? What their choices are? We have heard a little about some research into older people's views. We can also look at the market to see if people who have money make different choices from people who have not. So is market choice a good way of looking at things? We can look at the demand for private sheltered accommodation and see that it is there. It is a popular form of accommodation with support. People are buying it; people are developing it. We know that people do actually make choices to move into care homes, it is not just about accepting a last resort.

Increasingly, an interesting area is the behaviour of people who are trying to stay at home and trying to do so by themselves, perhaps having given up on trying to find a way through the disabled facilities grants system or to access the services of an occupational therapist. People are opening a copy of *Yours* magazine or something similar and phoning up companies that provide assistive products like stair lifts. This is an unregulated arena, one where Age Concern has undertaken some research on the selling techniques employed by companies. As a consumer, if you phone up a company and say I would like a stair lift and a sales representative comes in to see you, as you have initiated that contact, you lose many of your consumer rights – because you have invited them in. The problem with looking at market functioning is that it is not a perfect market because consumers do not have the information, as we know, that they need to make those choices. They have very few rights.

People do not have many rights in residential care settings; they do not have security of tenure in care homes, a fact which is borne out when we have seen homes close. There is a lot of debate about what has happened to service providers in this area over recent years, but very little debate about the importance of the residents' situation in these circumstances, and the insecurities that this can cause. What this also shows is that, even if you are in the position of having some capital to try to make some choices, it is still very difficult to do that. The reason is partly, that, whatever the national picture, or whatever choice you are supposed to have, what really matters is location. The debate has been around the numbers of residential homes that are closing, but, actually, it should be much more around what is happening locally and regionally. Is the supply meeting demand in particular areas?

We know that location is one factor influencing whether sheltered housing is hard to let. I think what we need to look at, in looking at the national policy in relation to the local situation, is locality commissioning for a range of housing and care options. We need the national policy framework to enable that to happen. For older people it may not be so much what the national policy is or what the supposed choice is. If you are in an area where a decision is made to build an eighty-bed nursing home, available staff from the local area will be drawn into one form of provision making it even more difficult to recruit people to other forms of services. It may actually limit choices to develop other services and find the staff available to do it. Some local authorities are looking at more creative approaches, and talking not just with health and social services, but also with housing, with community safety partnerships, transport and leisure groups and older people themselves. They are asking what people want, what mix of services they require and trying to develop a commissioning approach that will enable it to happen. The fact that some local authorities are able to do this suggests that the national policy framework does enable it to happen, but perhaps they are working against the tide rather than with it.

Finally, looking at the different policy impacts, regulation is a key aspect at a number of different levels. We have the Care Standards Act and the National Minimum Standards for Care Homes, which have attracted and continue to attract controversy. The government is not showing any great passion for introducing them in the way they were intended. It is soft peddling on a number of them. This sends out very poor messages. We have been hearing a good deal about expectations and about people moving into care and that their expectations are being met, or that homes had bettered or exceeded their expectations. What we also know is that people have very low expectations of what they were going to get, so one would hope that they were exceeded.

The changed definition of what is considered to be a registered home in the Care Standards Act has created some uncertainty about whether extra care housing constitutes a care home or housing provision. On the one hand, you have got government seeming to give backing to these forms of accommodation and care, but another part of government is actually throwing up a lot of uncertainty around whether or not extra care should be registered as a care home.

One of the key points here is that it will affect the vision of what extra care housing is about, but more importantly, it will affect individuals in those settings, because you will have the security of a tenancy agreement if you are in extra care housing versus being in a care home. Also, if you are in extra care housing, you have your disposable income. You purchase and pay for what you want. If you are in a care home, you receive a weekly allowance, which is sometimes referred to as 'pocket money'. This has a huge impact in terms of being able to exercise both choice and any kind of independence.

In some areas there is a driver for change. It has led some authorities to review the role of sheltered housing and to review day care services. And I think it does give some opportunity to think more flexibly about the type of services people might want. A policy initiative entitled 'Supporting People' is being introduced (April 2003); a very complex system. Enormous energy is being spent on recruiting a new group of people called *supporting people managers* and advisors. It is not likely to have a major impact on older people in the first year or two in terms of where the money is channelled, but further down the line, if one is feeling optimistic, it will make a positive difference, though it may need some more flexibility built in. If one is feeling pessimistic, it will just lead to providers of sheltered housing digging in their heels and trying to keep the funding directed towards sheltered housing.

We must not forget the role of 'direct payments'. I raise this because it was one of the big initiatives about giving people choice and control and yet, once again, it is an example of a lack of follow through from government, as with the care home standards. It's just not happening on any significant scale. This is important because these direct payments could begin to get people to question the culture of the way care is provided. At the very least, agencies need to think about the way they provide services, to try to give people as much control as possible.

Finally, age discrimination. This currently exists both in terms of government policies and at local policy level. So there is direct discrimination. There is also a good deal of indirect age discrimination. I think the tide is beginning to turn and June 2002 saw the launch, from Help the Aged, of their excellent 'Scrap It' campaign about raising public awareness about what age discrimination is. I believe the move to combat age discrimination will provide some sort of driver for change, and should also be used to challenge some of the assumptions around what is good enough for older people.

To conclude, one of the problems in terms of national policy is that there is not really a clear direction for commissioners and providers of services for older people. I think this is problematic in terms of future planning; we need to look at how we can actually enhance locality commissioning and provision of services. There is enough evidence to show that older people often do not want to move home but, if they do, they want to move within a very small radius – one or two miles. We do need to think about the local mix of services for older people. We do need to remember to address the issues for people who have got money and capital. I think there is sometimes a danger of saying if you have money then you can get on and mange on your own. Actually, we know no matter how much money you have, you'll never find it easy to find your way through the long term care systems. We ought to be thinking about better provision of information. As groups of experts struggle to make sense of 'Supporting People' we must question public understanding of the complex web of policy in this sphere. We have got to think of more ways of being able to get information across to older people so that they can make choices and have the information they need.

When we are looking at policy frameworks and funding frameworks it seems that there ought to be funding incentives that follow what older people tell us they want, rather than funding incentives, which at the moment simply highlight the kind of political sensitivity that government has. For example, there is current funding to deal with delayed discharge in hospitals, which is very good, but when the spotlight is removed, have we really looked at building capacity in social care sectors and the housing sectors? Have we really looked at developing the preventative services that older people need to remain in control of their own living arrangements?

COMMENTARY 2
Kalyani Gandhi

I'm going to expand on some of the issues raised in Isobel Allen's paper, in particular that of choice, and to approach this very much from a practitioner's point of view, rather than that of an academic researcher. I shall focus a little on how some of the choices that are made available are experienced by older people from minority ethnic groups, whether the choices are the same or, if not, what the differences are, and what the issues are in attempting to meet their needs and expectations. Isobel described at length the whole issue of 'need' and how 'need' has become so much a focus amongst assessment processes for older people.

I shall try to take the debate beyond 'need' and challenge the idea of need being applied across the board and looking at what older people's needs and older people's expectations are, over and above those which we tend to see very much as physically orientated in relation to services. We don't actually spend much time on developing sensitive assessment processes to take sufficient account of older people's expectations.

My experience comes from dealing with predominantly South Asian communities in London and the work carried out by the Eastwards Trust there. In terms of the background of the communities, Isobel's contribution is very interesting because it throws some light on the kind of data available in mapping what older people would like and how they perceive old age, in terms of motivation; feeling tired; wanting meals to be prepared for them; wanting to live in a group setting, and so on.

The Eastwards Trust works with immigrant communities, primarily the Asian population and predominantly first generation immigrants who came to this country around thirty years ago and who have grown up here. Most of these groups of people did not expect to remain living here and grow old in the UK, so their expectations of growing old in this country are very different to mainstream communities. However, over this thirty-year period people have become reconciled to the fact that they are not likely to be going back to their countries of origin. Their expectations vary, both their physical needs and their intellectual and emotional responses to the realisation that they might spend their final years in a country that was not their place of birth. As an example, in my professional capacity, I attend a lot of funerals. I try to meet the families of the former tenants. One of the most recent one's I attended was that of a woman from a Sri Lankan community, who came to the UK as a result of the longstanding conflict in Sri Lanka. She had been in this country for twelve years as a refugee and remained under refugee status as she grew older. In anticipation of her death, she had written her own memorial speech for the family to read out when at her funeral. They read it out when she was being cremated, and one of the things that she said was her greatest satisfaction in dying so far away from home, to which she had become reconciled, was the fact that her preferred lifestyle was to a great extent able to be realised.

She tried throughout the time she lived in the UK to tailor her lifestyle to conform to that which she had lived back home in Sri Lanka. She was expecting to be able to live in the UK, very close to the ways people used to live before she left Sri Lanka. That this was achievable comes down to a careful consideration of her expectations.

It is understandably a very difficult service for anyone to provide because you are talking about great diversity, a range of varying cultural needs and languages, a range of political reasons, and differing socio-economic status within communities. People expect to be able to have the same kind of family structures, responses from their own family and the carer networks, from the community around them as they might in their countries of origin.

In the nine years the Eastwards Trust has operated sheltered housing schemes I believe only one person has moved out to residential care, and that was a very acute case, where the person had to go because they were very frail indeed. The take-up of this form of care is very low because people do not identify the setting as something that is familiar to them, in terms of their expectations of possible support options.

What is it that people from minority ethnic groups really want? The term itself is not particularly helpful as a description of very diverse groups of people. Nevertheless it is a question being asked by both central and local government alike, as their communities are frequently poorly served and under-represented in the take-up of social services.

I shall restrict myself to using the term South Asian because that is the community I work with, many of the issues being raised, however, are pertinent to other minority communities. These people want to maintain family links. There is a whole different culture of ageing amongst South Asian communities than the more familiar western view of ageing, and although many are second generation immigrants who have been born here, they still have the cultural perspective that old age is actually a part of ones life where a range of concerns that could not be attended to in earlier stages of life, because one was doing myriad household duties, raising a family, etc, are to be addressed. It is a time for spiritual reconciliation, a time for preparation for death, and a time for taking stock about the course of ones life, fulfilling duties to one's family and friends and moving one step higher in personal self-achievement and self-evaluation. It is not seen culturally and philosophically within this culture as a point where life necessarily ends.

A lot of social care provision does not account for these kind of spiritual elements so important to members of South Asian, Hindu, Muslim, and Sikh religions. The rites and rituals that accompany this process of ageing are not recognised and provisions are not made for them. In line with this, most want to live within their own communities. There is an issue of joint family structures breaking down, for a number of reasons, but often due to the inadequate size of available housing, not least property prices in the current economic climate.

What we have found is that even though the initial constraints preventing families from living together cannot be overcome, people still want to maintain those links quite closely and quite regularly – it is not periodic or seasonal contact, families usually maintain daily contact. When services are offered an important question to this community becomes, who is offering it and how do they exercise any kind of control over those choices which are to be made?

Language is a big barrier; we tend to take it for granted but we don't understand the dynamics of how much of a barrier it can be when you are trying to understand the options that are available to you, be it sheltered housing; residential care; moving into a private home; or buying a house. Many older people in these communities are not able to read or write, this makes it very difficult to engage with them or for them to exercise their rights. This applies also to their own advocates, and their own family who may be advocating on their behalf.

One of the aims of Eastwards Trust can be illustrated by way of a case scenario. Eastwards Trust started off providing housing as an organisation when there was a lack of sheltered housing for Asian elders in East London. Over the last twenty years we have discovered that providing the housing and all the care support for older people that we can, is not enough. What these people do want is the chance to participate in the same kind of leadership that they held in their lives as family members in their community in this environment as well. To be respected, to have an active role in mentoring the younger generation in their own community, and within other organisations, be they temples or mosques.

How can this be facilitated? We must move beyond the provision of purely 'needs' based care, with its over dependence on the physical. One of the ways the Eastwards Trust is attempting to address this is by embarking upon an extensive training and education project, initially as a pilot project, conducting a series of older learning programmes to address the high levels of illiteracy amongst South Asian communities, particularly amongst women and even more so amongst older women. The training and education programmes cover basic skills, literacy and numeracy, providing them with an opportunity to either continue learning more or to engage in a range of opportunities within in their own communities.

An illustration, using housing as an example, of how people have reported their feelings to me is the perception of one's home (whether it is residential or sheltered) as an island. It is not an island of their making, and everybody else in the wider world comes in little boats, bringing whatever they think fit to take to the island. A bridge is never built, that could be there for them to use whenever they may wish to. What the Trust has been trying do is start building such a bridge, and leave the mechanisms open for people themselves to decide when and how they want to engage and about what. It is also a way of challenging the passive view of ageing, that ageing is not just a process. Of course our body ages physically and begins to slow down, but this doesn't necessarily mean a slowing down of all activities. I am not advocating that everybody has to and will take up all these opportunities, but it is likely that those who do, will then influence others with whom they live. One of the reasons we have not advocated setting up specialist homes for Asian elders with dementia or non-acute residential care is because it creates environments where there is no clear community support, where families can live together, or in very close proximity, support each other and break the sole dependency on the service provider.

In terms of available choices, a range of options does exist, at least in theory, but there are big problems in accessing these choices. The assessment processes which function as gate-keeping devices are notoriously complex not least because to access services one may have to deal with social services departments, housing departments, and health trusts to name only the main players. Without giving people the information they need to understand those choices, it is very difficult to exercise them.

I recently attended a meeting convened by the National Housing Federation, and it was very difficult as a group of professionals to understand the implications of the current developments within the housing and care arenas. One of the comments made when discussing the implementation of the 'supporting people programme', was when are we going to engage service users in this debate? The answer was that until we are clear, we can't tell them. That says it all. What it is important to do, and what is needed, is to break older people's dependency on other people making decisions for them and continuously acting on their behalf, partly through the provision of gateways to greater self-sufficiency through engagement.

To conclude, I would just like to say that, for myself, and for most people that I have worked with, there is a very big difference between needs and wants. We tend to blur the definition between the two and assume they are the same thing. In fact they are very different and one must not dismiss what a person wants on the grounds of resource constraints, because then you are never actually fulfilling your responsibility or you are never going to achieve the standards and independence that is wanted both by older people and is trumpeted by policy.

6 Choosing and managing your own community in later life

Maria Brenton

Introduction

Most people would say that a reasonably acceptable formula for old age is to be able to enjoy privacy in your own home, to have company near at hand when you want it and to rely on the security of familiar neighbours if you need help. For those who live alone, the majority of whom are older women, these elements are especially important and they are therefore a group to whom the idea of a co-housing community often has a special appeal. For older couples, too, co-housing offers the assurance that the surviving partner will be able to continue living among familiar and supportive neighbours. Staying healthy, happy and active in old age, maintaining your autonomy and participating in a co-operative enterprise with people you have chosen to live with are the principal objectives of the co-housing community.

The Older Women's CoHousing project

The Older Women's CoHousing (OWCH) Company Ltd is a pilot project aiming to adapt to the British context a model of group living developed by older Dutch people and extensively researched in a study for the Housing Corporation (Brenton 1998).

Based in London, the OWCH group set up their project in mid-1998 in order to plan a life together as a community in one building. The group elected from the start to remain a 'women-only' group, but their experience is relevant for groups of men and women. Their intention has always been to offer a model that could be replicated by other older people. In this aim, they have been supported by the Joseph Rowntree Foundation who have funded a part-time consultant for the group (Maria Brenton). Support and encouragement has also come from the Housing Corporation, which is interested in their intended mix of owners, shared owners and social renters. The Corporation, having funded the original study of Dutch co-housing communities of older people (Brenton 1998) has also funded a study into the legal and financial feasibility of co-housing communities, using the OWCH group as a test case. Supplementary funding from the Social Housing Grant has been agreed in principle to finance the rented elements in the scheme when it is built. The search for a possible site is currently in progress.

What exactly is co-housing?

The term 'CoHousing Community' was coined by two American architects (McCamant and Durrett 1994) to convey a form of collaborative living developed in Denmark and copied extensively in North America and in other European counties (but not in Britain).

What makes co-housing distinct from other ways of living is that its members choose to form an 'intentional community' and to combine individual or family privacy with group living. The whole point of doing this is that they first get to know each other in order to live as a group. A number of features need to be noted:

- Because accommodation for each social unit is self-contained, the group could not be termed a commune.

- It may resemble a housing co-operative but it will differ from many such groups because the essential distinguishing feature of a co-housing community is that its members live on one specific site with the aim of sharing common activities and common space.

- It may resemble a sheltered housing complex – the difference is that the co-housing community is set up and run by its members. In fact, it could offer a model for 'doing sheltered housing differently'.

- The group controls its own affairs and takes decisions corporately.

● How far members live in common is a matter for choice and thus will vary from group to group.

● Entry to the group is governed by a desire to live as part of the group and conform to its ethos and rules.

Co-housing communities of older people

Co-housing communities of older people have developed in the Netherlands, Denmark and to some extent in Germany. These groups have chosen to be child-free and to confine membership to people over the age of 50 years. Most of them consist of married couples and single women – but there are some groups with single women only. An important condition for membership is a commitment to mutual support within the group – defined as everyday neighbourly assistance rather than as a replacement for professional care services. In the Netherlands and Denmark, older people do have the option of joining or helping to form an intergenerational group of families, couples and singles. Those who choose to live with their age-peers do so for a number of reasons, not least of which is that they prefer a quiet and peaceful environment. Their interests and life-experiences may also coincide to a greater degree than in an intergenerational setting.

The Dutch and Danish governments have actively encouraged the development of 'Living Groups' by older people in the belief that they keep older people happier, healthier and more active than they might otherwise have been. This may mean reduced demand on health and social services care and support. There is some research evidence in Britain (Kingston *et al.* 2001) to suggest that living with one's peers has distinct advantages in 'maintaining health status'. Reflecting on their comparisons of older people living in a retirement community with those in a wider community sample, the authors comment that 'age-specific living, when accompanied by a culture of peer support, has emerged as a powerful aid to morale and an antidote to age-prejudice'.

In the Netherlands, local authorities and housing associations view co-housing as a form of social investment for older people and they assist the process in many practical ways. The local authorities help with planning permission and sometimes with cheaper land or redundant buildings. Often, in the larger cities, groups of older people get the help of a part-time development worker funded by the local authority or sometimes a housing association takes the initiative and reaches out to older people to encourage them to get organised. Most of the nearly 200 existing and intending groups in the Netherlands (VROM 1998) have been helped to develop within the social housing sector – a sector which is broader and more generous than in Britain. There is a long tradition of rental tenure among the Dutch, although this is changing. Newly emerging groups nowadays tend to have a mix of rental and owner occupation. Where rental is concerned, housing associations cede the landlord's role of allo- cating tenancies to the groups themselves. Within certain agreements and safeguards about voids, the groups choose who comes to fill a vacancy. They generally operate a waiting list of would-be members whom the group has got to know over time by involving them in social and other events.

There is in the Netherlands a national network of Older People's 'Living Groups' with a regional structure. Those wishing to form a group or to identify one to join can look to this organ- isation for assistance. There is also a strong tradition of shared learning between existing groups and new ones.

Some key dimensions of co-housing are:

● community of place

● community of interest

● community development

● autonomy and capacity building

● choice of new members and succession

● a physical design which facilitates social interaction

'Community of place'

The attraction of co-housing for some thousands of people with an age range of 50 to 90+ years in the Netherlands lies in its ready-made companionability, the scope for stimulus and activity that it offers and the security of living in a small-scale neighbourhood or 'community of place' where everyone knows everyone else.

Older people tend to spend more time in their homes than younger groups. Sometimes over their lifetime they have watched their old neighbourhoods change with the steady transfer of homes from an old to a younger generation. Where they once knew their neighbours and could therefore rely on them for support in an emergency, now their locality may have become more anonymous and perhaps hostile. Peopled by young families, it may also be virtually empty during the day. By contrast, being part of a co-housing community means that there are always people on hand whom you know, who are 'the eyes on the street' and who will notice if you do not appear to get up one morning. This provides a strong sense of security, remarked on by many older co-housing members (Brenton 1998).

'Community of interest'

'Community of place', where people have a sense of belonging to a group in a particular building or locality, combines with 'community of interest' in co-housing groups. At the very least, what brings people together and binds them is an active shared interest in living as part of the group, for whatever underlying motives. Sometimes an added unifier might be ethnic identity, culture or religion – or it might be simply an interest shared by many of the members in something like gardening or rambling. Groups tend to form and recruit at first from the natural networks of the early initiators of the project and shared interests are the foundation of many networks. The most successful groups are felt to be those in which people who join do so from a positive wish to contribute to the joint enterprise and to partic-ipate in joint activities. Where someone's dominant motive springs from loneliness, dependency or an inability to be alone, he or she may not find the answer to such needs in the group.

Community development

The most important building block of a co-housing community is the gradual development of a sense of group identity and cohe-sion in advance of having a building. The message of Dutch co-housing members is 'Build the group first. Don't be in a hurry. Above all, don't get into a situation where you have to recruit new members in a hurry. You will live to regret it.'

When a group comes together at the start to plan a co-housing community, a great deal of energy and time input is required to get it off the ground and therefore a core at least of participants need to be relatively fit and energetic. The development process takes resolve, determination and optimism. In order to 'grow' the group around a shared aim, participants have to sort out with each other where they are coming from and where they wish to arrive. In other words, they have to articulate their own basic values and measure them against those of other people to seek out and identify common ground, particularly in relation to agreeing a balance between individual and group living. This process contributes either to the cementing of some basic bonds or a parting of the ways. Some participants will decide along the way that group living is not for them and select themselves out or be encouraged by others to leave the group. By the end of a long period of meeting and planning (typically, in the Netherlands, four years) participants know each other fairly well and know if there is sufficient common ground for them to go ahead and live as a group. Even so, a national study of older people's co-housing groups in the Netherlands found that 'Many groups felt with hindsight that too little attention had been paid to the group formation in the initiative phase' (VROM 1998, p. 29).

The principle of mutual support, its meaning and limits, is much discussed in the planning stages before people commit to the group. Mutual support is the formal expression of a reciprocity that will grow naturally over time as people get to know each other in the process of building the group.

Capacity building

According to Fromm in her study of collaborative living, 'The development process is the training ground for resident management' (1991, p.159). The task of developing a co-housing community demands the exercise of a range of skills and competences. Participants have to find their way around the local political environment; they have to be able to convince local politicians that they are a serious and reliable enterprise; they have to find either a housing association to assist them or a commercial developer; they have to be able to set out their agreed preferences and requirements. In terms of the organisation of the group, a minimum of committee and communication skills is needed, formal procedures have to be established and records kept. Participants have to be aware of the need for group building, for reaching a basis for mutual agreement on ends and means. They have to be able to cope with inevitable conflicts emerging within the group. Finally, once their building is ready for occupation, they have to be able to manage and maintain it collectively, deal with its finances and order the affairs of the group.

Choice of new members

Succession is a key issue for a co-housing group. It is vital for the integrity and smooth running of the group that when a member dies or moves away, the vacant place can be filled by someone who is reasonably compatible with the remaining members and who will subscribe to the ethos of the group. A careful process of recruitment and selection is needed. A long vacancy can also be costly to the group financially. Through the waiting list, applicants are known already to the group. There may be an informal vetting process, a home visit to the applicant, and interviews with representatives of the group before a decision is made.

When a new recruit moves in, he or she is joining a group that is already established and this is a very different matter from being in there at the start as one of the pioneers, sharing the discussions and contributing to the process. The entry problem of the new member is recognised in many of the Dutch groups as one that the group needs to have measures to address if the transition is to be successful and the new member integrated into the group.

Physical design

Many of the Danish and North American family-based co-housing communities have been designed by their inhabitants to resemble something like a small hamlet of houses around a communal space that is car-free and child-friendly. They will have a common house which may accommodate a communal kitchen and dining room, a laundry, a shop, teenagers' rumpus room, a crèche and office space. Meals are often held in common. Mail will be delivered to a central point so that people will meet as they go to collect it. In the Netherlands older people's 'living groups' are generally built as blocks of flats – often around an atrium or a garden – with front doors facing onto each other and circulation routes planned so that people will meet. Communal space is a standard feature of older people's accommodation in the Netherlands but in 'living groups' it is often more generous, to accommodate residents'

interests and guest space. Older people frequently participate in
the design process for their building – a possibility enhanced by
the flexibility of Dutch design and construction methods.

Conclusion: Dutch experience

In the Netherlands, a route map already exists to guide a group of
older people who wish to develop a co-housing community.
Intending groups in the Netherlands can take advantage of a
wealth of guidance and information from the prior experience of
other groups over a period of twenty years. The national organisation supplies guidelines and advice. Existing groups can be
visited and their mistakes learned from. There is also in the
Dutch policy environment a climate of recognition and acceptance and an official willingness to assist what they are aiming for.
An intending group can take advantage of courses available in
community education on group living and conflict resolution.
They can often obtain local authority funding for bringing in a
consultant or trainer to coach them on group living. Apart from
all this wealth of available assistance, however, a forming group
still generally has much to learn, new skills to develop and old
ones to polish up.

The OWCH project's relevance to older people

Like its Dutch counterparts, the Older Women's CoHousing
project challenges prevailing stereotypes of old age. This is the
group's declared intention. Aware that there is little tradition in
Britain of the active initiation of residential projects by older
people themselves, this group of older women decided to start
one. In setting out on this path, they have rejected the options
currently on offer to older people in Britain – or they are saying
at least that some of these could be set up differently.

Specialist housing for older people, where it exists, is generally
the preserve of the commercial developer, social landlords or
charitable bodies. The older person in need of accommodation
offering accessibility, companionship, support and care is usually
cast as a passive consumer in a 'top down' rather than 'bottom
up' system. This does not have to be the case. The OWCH project
is a practical demonstration of the energy and resolve to be
found among older people in sorting out their own solutions in
advance of the needs of increasing old age. This is a group with
the clear goal of sustaining individual autonomy and control

over their living arrangements. The project has attracted interest from many older people around the country – particularly from older women living alone and seeking a group to join in their own area.

How co-housing fits with British housing policy

The philosophy of the OWCH group, with its emphasis on autonomy and individual choice is reflected in current government policy on older people's housing, emphasising choice, participation and diversity. According to *Quality and Choice for Older People's Housing* (DETR/DH 2001) a strategic approach to older people's housing should be 'integrated, holistic, inclusive, involving and preventative'. Co-housing delivers on all these policy objectives.

> Housing is much more than just the bricks and mortar. It determines people's identity, their privacy, space and the place where they express their individuality. It is one of the determining factors in promoting the independence of older people, wherever they choose to live.
>
> (DETR/DH 2001)

Prevention

In the seminar series on which this book is based, governmental stress on keeping older people in their own homes has been raised as an issue for concern, on the grounds that isolation in the home can often be more damaging to older people than moving to residential alternatives. Co-housing is about keeping your own home and privacy but moving to a different setting to live with people you know. It is also a major exercise in prevention. Social services departments tend to target resources almost exclusively on the high-dependency end of the age-spectrum to the neglect of younger old people. Co-housing for older people, on the other hand, embraces a range of ages above fifty years and consists primarily of people who can sustain themselves and are willing to support each other in independent living. To an extent, they keep each other healthy. Living in a co-housing community only remains attractive and workable if the dependency balance is kept viable – which is not necessarily a factor of age per se. The co-housing community does not substitute for residential care or a nursing home but it can delay or prevent entry to either. It is not necessarily a last stop for older people but, where adequate local care and support services can be made available to people in their homes, there is the added dimension of willing neighbour support along with companionship and shared activities.

Co-housing is about 'joined-up' thinking. It requires an integrated perspective which recognises the importance of housing and a sense of community for keeping older people active, involved, happy and healthy and therefore perhaps reducing demand on health and social services expenditure. It caters for the immediate and future needs of people who would otherwise live alone – and there are growing numbers of single householders in our society, 'over two in every five people born between 1946 and 1950 will be living alone by the age of 75' (Falkingham 1997, p. 37). Older women are a specific group for whom co-housing offers immeasurable advantages.

Women living alone

The gender difference in living alone in old age is striking. Three quarters of older people living alone are women (Leather 1999). People of this age group living alone are heavily over-represented in council and housing association accommodation. Of older people who do not live alone, the vast majority (69 per cent) live with other older people, most of them with only one other person in a couple.

Older women in London

An estimated 663,000 older women live in London. They form 57 per cent of people aged 60 and over, 64 per cent of those aged 75 and over and 73 per cent of those aged 85 and over. 1991 census figures show that women form 78 per cent of the lone person households over 60 in London (Belcher and Field 2001).

How co-housing does not fit with British housing practice

Co-housing, more than twenty years old in the Netherlands, offers a model which would seem to fit today's policy priorities in Britain. I have argued elsewhere that co-housing constitutes a form of living likely to appeal to the post-war baby boom generation who have grown up with higher expectations of choice and autonomy than their forebears (Brenton 1999, 2001). It has particular appeal to women who have been influenced by the 1970s women's movement and who are now growing old. What then stands in its way in this country? A number of factors may be listed, some of them self-evident and others which need to be explored briefly here:

- co-housing's lack of familiarity to housing providers and housing finance institutions;

- the rigidities of owner occupation;

- the paternalism of the social housing sector;

- the relative passivity of older people;

- the conflict between tenant choice and local authority nominations;

- the shortage and inflated costs of land and housing, particularly in London and major cities;

- the dominance of a limited range of models for older people such as sheltered housing, residential care, etc.

The housing sector

The Older Womens CoHousing group's experience since 1998 shows that the autonomy of a co-housing scheme is not readily recognised, taken up or promoted by the British political system or the housing market. Both the housing and social care sectors have a long tradition of paternalism in relation to older people. The attitudes of housing professionals can be fixed and negative. Local authorities remain relatively impenetrable to direct participation and are burdened – in London especially – with a heavy legacy of family homelessness and housing shortage. The housing needs of families have been predominant over the last fifty years (Bernard and Phillips 1998) and older people's needs are not high priority. The dominance of owner occupancy in Britain, the poor condition and age of much of the housing stock and the residual role of the social housing sector makes for clear differences when compared with the Netherlands. However, there is a policy trend in Britain towards encouraging tenant management and choice in the social housing sector. As noted earlier, at the beginning of the twenty-first century government policy is to encourage diversity, empowerment and choice in older people's housing (DETR/DH 2001).

British culture and older people

Were it not for the existence of the OWCH group and the interest it has attracted from older people around the country, it might be concluded that older people in Britain are and are seen as an unlikely population group to embark on the task of developing a co-housing community. Institutional ageism predominates in housing as in other areas and can be internalised by older people themselves (Bytheway 1995, Minichiello *et al.* 2000). The prevailing image of old age in the popular consciousness is one of vulnerability and dependency because the needs of frail older people for support services colours general perceptions of old age (Means and Smith 1998). Yet the vast majority of older people live independently and have little recourse to social services. Audit Commission figures show that among people aged 85 and upwards, over half (58 per cent) live independently in their own homes without formal community health and social services support. A further 18 per cent live in their own homes with this support (1996 figures, Audit Commission 1997).

In the UK there are not many older people's activist groups lobbying for change. The national older people's pension movement focuses exclusively on the state pension, which, although a key determinant of housing chances, is only one facet of public policy. Most older people's organisations are run for them by others. There is no tradition of older people's unions or politics or protest as there is in the Netherlands. The older population in Britain has yet to realise the strength and significance of its voting power. The lively assertiveness of the OWCH group stands out against this unfavourable background of old age passivity, but they are not unique. There clearly is demand among older people for co-housing where they recognise the term – or for its benefits, where they do not.

How is co-housing different from current housing provisions for older people?

The question needs to be asked: 'Are there housing arrangements already available to older people in Britain that can offer all the features supplied by a co-housing community?'

In summary these features are:

- the group is set up by its members;

- group cohesion is fostered by the initial development process;

- members choose to live together in order to get to know the other members of the group and because they wish to live as members of the group;

- members make a commitment to mutual support;

- the group is controlled and managed by its members;

- the group takes decisions democratically;

- the group has its own distinct legal status;

- the group is able to select new members and therefore to try to maintain a balance of ages, a degree of compatibility within the group and a commitment to mutual support and participation;

- individual members have their own self-contained space and privacy and choice of how much to participate;

- the group shares some common activities, common space and facilities.

A retirement community, sheltered housing or an Abbeyfield community as they are currently organised in Britain would offer some of these features but are generally established and run by third parties for rather than by older people. Older people can choose to live in them but have little choice about whom they live with nor are allocations necessarily based on considerations of compatibility, common interests or support of a common endeavour.

Choice and the social housing sector

Although experiments in consumer choice of housing are being conducted in various pilot projects in Britain which seek to replicate and adapt the Dutch Delft housing model, it cannot be said that the principle of choice for people *without* purchasing power is embedded in the British system. Quite the opposite. Receipt of public money traditionally means the denial or limitation of choice. This principle has a long history in nineteenth-century definitions of the 'deserving poor' and 'less eligibility' for the workhouse – direct antecedents of today's social services and social housing.

People are not generally eligible for social housing unless they conform to a narrow definition of housing need, particularly in areas of housing pressure – although where older and disabled people are concerned other needs such as health and vulnerability will be taken into account. Social housing tenants often have little choice of where they live. It is also the custom for local authorities to make nominations for a significant proportion of any social housing development. How far other needs such as that for companionship, social validation and a sense of belonging are also defined as such and given weight in housing allocations is an open question. Of course, housing-need-based allocations have validity in the context of housing shortage – but the question needs to be asked – 'for how many decades can the excuse of shortage of supply be allowed to deny choice?' Beyond this, the lack of a range of alternative options for barrier-free housing suitable for older people is in itself a major constraint on choice for people who are not in a position to buy what they want. The lack of an option of two bedrooms similarly constrains choice and restricts quality of life for older people and makes a nonsense of policies aimed at rapid turnover in hospital care and family care and support at home.

Even less does the system recognise that social housing tenants who share a building and living arrangements with others in a communal setting might wish to express a preference about whom they live with. An allocation system based purely on narrowly defined need – which is a rationing system driven by cost – does not easily accommodate issues of compatibility, shared interests, shared culture, support of certain values or the wish to be part of a specific group – all of which contribute to a sense of community and group cohesion.

It was noted earlier that an essential element of a co-housing community is the selection of members who want to be part of it and are genuinely motivated to live according to its ethos and norms. That to some extent they know and are known by existing members before they move in is a key to its success. Such a selection process is never foolproof – but has more chance of contributing to a sense of community than a random allocation process exercised by some external authority on criteria totally unrelated to how someone might fit into the life of the group. Without the ability to select members for a broad adherence to the aims of the group, there is no point in having co-housing.

What would otherwise distinguish it from any warden-less sheltered housing complex?

Equal opportunities

In my work trying to build up on behalf of the OWCH group an understanding and climate of acceptance of co-housing among housing providers, this principle of selection based on resident choice has often met with hostility. The first question raised is 'How does allowing tenants to allocate tenancies conform to equal opportunities? They would favour all their friends and keep out anyone they don't happen to like.' I don't have any clear answers to this save to point out that here we have a conflict between two positive values – choice and non-discrimination – where one appears to cancel out the other.

Does a solution lie in the kind of criteria upon which a choice is to be exercised? If I want to keep you out of a group because you are black or gay or disabled – that is clearly wrong. If you wish to live in a group that has been set up to pursue specific and legitimate aims but do not intend to or cannot subscribe to those aims, why should the fact that it receives public subsidy entitle you to a place? A youth club would not have to accept members as old as 40 or 60, for example. To do so would negate its purpose. Why then should housing based on co-operation have to accept people who may not have the slightest desire to co-operate?

The OWCH group and choice

The OWCH group wishes to exercise choice in admitting to membership (and tenancies):

- women;
- women over the age of 50 years;
- women not requiring regular assistance from the group which should properly be sought from social care services;
- women who are actively committed to the group's values and willing to participate in its activities;
- women who have attended at least three OWCH meetings and who have been on a waiting list for at least six months;
- women who qualify for a particular category of dwelling.

Training in equal opportunities

There is of course a need to exercise great vigilance in relation to discriminatory practice. The OWCH group's literature welcomes women from 'any background or culture'. Its members wish to create an environment where 'all women have equal voice and are valued equally irrespective of class, ethnicity, belief, disability and sexual preference'. They are keen to target black and minority ethnic women's groups for recruitment. The age-structure of these populations is younger and for some groups there is a strong preference for living with family members (Belcher and Field 2001). The OWCH group has sought funding for and undertaken specialist training on diversity and equal opportunities, covering the Sex Discrimination Act, the Race Relations Act and the Disability Discrimination Act. They are likely to be 'scrutinised for diversity' on the grounds of race but they already represent an unusual socio-economic mix and embrace a wide range of physical and mental health impairments. Their restriction of the group to women only may also be subject to criticism but can be supported on a number of grounds, not least that older women are themselves an oppressed and vulnerable minority.

The group itself writes:

One of the most important of our early decisions was to be a women-only group. The reasons for this were:

● *the majority of older people are women and they are most likely to be on their own in old age;*

● *culturally, in our age group, men tend to dominate and to have different attitudes to co-operation and mutual support;*

● *we wanted to help change the ageist image of older women as passive and dependent;*

● *we wanted to develop and enhance general confidence and skills and the quality of life among older women;*

● *we felt that the personal care we would sometimes need to give each other would be easier if we were all women.*

Local authority nominations

Apart from arguments about equal opportunities, a major impediment to the group's exercise of choice of members may lie in local authority nomination rights and a strict adherence to 'housing need'. It is to be hoped that a local authority will, like its Dutch counterparts, look on the OWCH community as a positive investment and a development to be encouraged. The OWCH group's access in principle to a pan-London Social Housing Grant will mean that a local authority will not lose out on any normal entitlements. An arrangement that will both support the group's freedom to choose its members and meet local authority housing pressures is perfectly possible. The group can recruit women from the housing register or from existing social housing tenants as long as the local authority allows them a degree of tolerance in seeking a proper fit with OWCH criteria for membership.

Choice in design

The OWCH group also wishes to participate in the design of their dwelling and for over two years they have maintained a subgroup which has been tasked to look into desirable design features and energy efficiency. They are keenly interested in an ecological approach to housing and in sharing resources such as transport, bulk order deliveries and household equipment such as washing machines. The task-group has thought long and hard about the environment they consider appropriate to ageing. They want light and airy rooms, movable internal walls, access to external space through balconies and a shared garden and space for meeting each other and pursuing crafts and other interests. They want some thought to go into their circulation space so that it is easy to meet each other as they come in and out. They want their accommodation to be barrier-free and wheelchair accessible, with appropriate sound and heat insulation and storage.

Hopefully, the OWCH group will have an opportunity to participate in the design of their dwelling. However, standard designs, tight cost and profit margins and the unfamiliarity of architects and developers with consumer participation are all factors which may prevent this highly desirable input.

Conclusion

The OWCH project

The Older Women's CoHousing group has a mix of owners and renters but is a predominantly low income group. As with many older women, some of the owner occupiers can be said to be 'capital rich and cash poor' and a number of them may need to realise capital for future income. The planned mixed tenure of the OWCH group promises an inclusive and sustainable community in one building that is relatively unusual in our highly segregated society. The project has highlighted the gulf that exists between the choices available to those who have purchasing power and the lack of choice for those who have not, where 'beggars can't be choosers'. This is not a function of being old, but of being poor – but to be old and a woman on your own means you are quite likely to be poor. Finding a site for the group is difficult, partly because there can be no automatic assumption that everyone will accept the lowest common denominator of social housing. There is in fact a salutary and understandable resistance on the part of the owner occupiers in the group to what they view as the low standards of amenity and environment associated with social housing. It is conceivable that the realities of the London housing market may force a degree of compromise on what they would ideally want but also that their expectations and financial input may result in an expansion of choice and quality for the social renters. As an OWCH member commented: 'An inclusive neighbourhood should mean levelling up, not down.'

The future

It will become clear in time whether the Older Women's CoHousing group manage to pioneer a different way of living for older people in Britain and establish a new housing option that is welcomed and supported by housing developers, social services and health care agencies. Interestingly, in the early 1980s a similar group of women in London set out on this same path and devoted much time and energy over the years to developing their own co-operative living arrangements. Traced in 1997 in the course of the author's research, these women, increasingly frail and aged from their early seventies to nineties, still, sadly, all lived alone. They had faced such difficulties and met so little encouragement or support, that they gave up. If, in five years from now, when their current oldest member will be aged 80 years, the women in OWCH are still living alone and scattered across the London boroughs, a great opportunity will have been missed, not just for them but for older people generally. The

OWCH women are working very hard to realise their co-housing community. What is also needed is imagination and flexibility from those agencies involved with older people's wellbeing and housing.

On a more optimistic note, the Older Women's CoHousing project has been seized upon with enthusiasm by the Greater London Authority as a possible model for new forms of living in London. The draft London Plan, issued by the Mayor of London in June 2002, exhorted London Boroughs to take an imaginative approach to developing mixed and balanced communities and to 'promote new concepts in urban living such as co-housing communities which are resident developed projects where mixed tenure homes are clustered around a common space with a range of shared facilities'. With this clear strategic guidance, it is to be hoped that the OWCH project will find the support it needs and pave the way for other groups of older people to exercise choice and take charge of their own living arrangements.

References

Audit Commission (1997) *The Coming of Age: improving care services for older people*, London: Audit Commission.

Belcher, Z and Field, S (2001) *Homes for London's Women*, London: Greater London Authority.

Bernard, M and Phillips, J (1998) *The Social Policy of Old Age: moving into the 21st century*, London: Centre for Policy on Ageing.

Brenton, M (1998) *'We're in charge'. CoHousing Communities of Older People in the Nederlands: lessons for Britain?*, Bristol: Policy Press.

Brenton, M (1999a) *Choice, Autonomy and Mutual Support: older women's collaborative living arrangements*, York: York Publishing Services/Joseph Rowntree Foundation.

Brenton, M (1999b) Co-operative living arrangements among older women, *Local Environment* 4(1)(February): 79–87.

Brenton, M (2001) Older people's CoHousing communities, in S Peace and C Holland (eds) *Inclusive Housing for an Ageing Society*, Bristol: Policy Press.

Bytheway, B (1995) *Ageism*, Buckingham: Open University Press.

DETR/DH (2001) *Quality and Choice for Older People's Housing: a strategic framework*, London: The Stationery Office.

Falkingham, J (1997) Who are the baby boomers? A demographic profile, in M Evandrou (ed.) *Baby Boomers: ageing in the 21st century*, London: Age Concern.

Fromm, D (1991) *Collaborative Communities: CoHousing, Central Living and other forms of new housing with shared facilities*, New York: Van

Nostrand Reinhold.

Kingston, P, Bernard, M, Biggs, S and Nettleton, H (2001) Assessing the health impact of age-specific housing, *Health and Social Care in the Community* 9(4): 228–234.

Leather, P (1999) *Age-File '99*, Kidlington: Anchor Research.

Means, R and Smith, R (1998) *From Poor Law to Community Care: the development of welfare services for elderly people 1939–1971*, Bristol: Policy Press.

McCamant, K and Durrett, C (1994) *CoHousing: a contemporary approach to housing ourselves*, Berkeley CA: Ten Speed Press.

Minichiello, V, Browne, J and Kendig, H (2000) Perceptions and consequences of ageism: views of older people, *Ageing and Society* 20(3) (May): 253–278.

VROM (1998) *Van Idealisme naar Realisme*, Zoetertneer: Ministerie van Volkshuisvesting, Ruimtefijke Ordening en Milieubeheer.

COMMENTARY 1

Steve Ongeri

Who's doing the choosing?

The Older Women's CoHousing project, so ably described by Maria Brenton, is an important touchstone in the development of housing choice for older people in England. The government has clearly signalled its interest in developing the range of housing options available, particularly in social housing. The Housing Green Paper and the government's framework for older people are clear signals of its commitment.

The Housing Corporation is also keen to increase the range of housing choices and this is one of the main reasons we have backed the Older Women's CoHousing project (OWCH) in their attempt to build a co-housing project in London. Our primary motivation is to increase the number of housing choices available to older people. Essentially, co-housing adds to the menu of choices available.

Why are we all interested in choice? At one level, we are interested in it because we see the right to choose as an extension of citizen's rights. For governments and providers, the exercise of choice is seen as one way in which those who pay rent or taxes can give something back for their investment. In June 2002, the government announced plans to introduce more choice into the

National Health Service. Although governments have sought to extend choice over the last decade or more, the idea does not seem to be the sole province of governments of any particular political shade. The previous government altered the balance between capital and revenue subsidies in social housing, on the grounds that revenue subsidy through housing benefit allowed individuals more choice where they lived.

Nursery vouchers, are another example of choice, but perhaps show that the liberation ostensibly offered by having the power in your own hands can quickly remove the pleasure from choosing. In the case of nurseries, markets have not been able to respond to parents exercising choice and many have quickly found themselves priced out of the market. In housing, the idea of a shopping incentive in housing benefit has not met with universal support. Some have voiced suspicions about policy makers' intentions in this area. Is this really offering more choice, or is the idea simply to persuade benefit recipients to move to cheaper areas, reducing the overall bill?

Nevertheless, the increase in choice in social housing in England has moved us away from the 'one offer and out' culture and the idea that professionals know best. Indeed, there are no signs so far that the choice agenda in housing has run its course. The government's plans for rent restructuring over the next ten years are aimed at enabling tenants to make choices based on a more rational, 'you get what you pay for', principle. Interest in choice based lettings continues, and at the Housing Corporation we are intending to introduce a choice based system for sheltered housing developed from a piece of work undertaken with the Elderly Accommodation Counsel (EAC) (2002).

It is always difficult to know how *real* choice is. For instance, owner occupiers' exercise of choice is bounded by some very real constraints. Generally speaking, it is conditioned by what they can afford. We now see older owner occupiers choosing rented sheltered housing because they want to move to a specific location, usually near friends and relatives, because they can't afford to move there as a purchaser.

Why though is a choice now such an issue for older people? Older people in social housing have the same sort of constraints placed on exercising their choice as tenants of all ages. There is some evidence that older people across Western Europe have been able to exercise even less choice than the general population. Work funded by the Corporation for the HOPE Network

(Riseborough 1998) can be summed up as saying that the participation of older people in housing decisions across Western Europe is patchy in the general stock and, in specialised housing, virtually non existent. In addition, we know from work on housing advice we have carried out with the Housing Associations Charitable Trust (hact) and Age Concern (1999) that, while many of the normal factors bounding housing choice still ring true for older people (especially location), they have some additional housing related factors to take into account. Examples might be community, security, social care and health issues.

We know from the 'hact' and Age Concern work, that these additional issues are not always taken into account by the professionals who advise others on housing. It is often difficult for older people and their relatives to make choices, because there is no simple route for finding out what choices are available in these important housing related areas. This clearly has an effect on who does the choosing. It implies that it is no good just increasing the range of items on the menu, without providing the tools by which people can exercise fair choice. The Housing Corporation is currently developing such a tool in the 'Bringing It All Together' project with EAC .

A choice is only fair and reasonable if people are empowered to make choices. There are excluded groups of older people who are even less empowered than most. Examples here might be older people in the countryside or black and minority ethnic older people. In these circumstances, outreach services are vital. Peddars Way Housing Association (now known as Flagship) undertook some outreach work with older people in Norfolk, funded by Anchor and the Housing Corporation (Cameron Harrison *et al.* 2000). The outreach scheme itself was successful, but some quite scary stories emerged. For many older people in rural north Norfolk, choice was not an issue, because they were not even aware that the menu of choices existed. Finally, work for the Corporation by the SAMEC Trust (Ali-Khan and Khan 1999) on black and minority ethnic older people and sheltered housing has shown that choice can be removed entirely if the menu does not contain what you actually want.

For housing providers, there are downsides to choice as well. There is a good deal of evidence that older people in sheltered housing have voted with their feet when better options turned up. It is well documented that older people are not interested in sheltered housing in unsafe or unwelcoming locations or those with very small accommodation, especially if there is something better available. We also have to be aware that those doing the choosing may make choices that we don't like and there needs to be a careful line drawn to define when this becomes inappropriate. The challenge is to develop policy and services which are centred on the individual, as opposed to tailoring services towards specific age groups.

What therefore does the work of the older women's co-housing project tell us about choice? First of all it has an optimistic message – if people want to add a particular choice, and they are prepared to work at it, they have a chance of getting that choice delivered, particularly now, when so many agencies from the government downwards agree that choice is an important issue. We can speculate that more older people will want to make lifestyle choices, to go to the seaside or the country perhaps and then perhaps to move back to where services are when they are older. Work carried out for the Corporation by Moyra Riseborough, Peter Fletcher and David Mullins (2001) has shown that there is an abiding demand for low/no care sheltered housing. We have already heard from Leonie Kellaher on how design and space issues affect the way in which older people choose housing.

However, there will continue to be boundaries placed by governments around the exercise of choice. The least we can expect is that these boundaries will be constantly reviewed. It is much less likely that specialised housing for older people will contain one-bedroom dwellings. Maria Brenton's paper draws attention to the way in which housing choice and equal opportunities can clash and also explains how the OWCH group developed an acceptable compromise between the two. This will always happen, because as in most areas of life, we cannot do all the choosing ourselves. In society people operate in an interdependent way and that means that our own choice will inevitably be constrained by the choices of others. This is particularly so where expenditure on housing is concerned. Owner occupiers can only expect what is affordable and so can social renters.

References

Age Concern and hact (1999) *Where Can I Go?*, London: Age Concern and hact.

Ali-Khan, M and Khan, S (1999) *Steps to Understanding: a good practice guide for registered social landlords to communicating with black and minority ethnic older people*, London: SAMEC Trust and the Housing Corporation.

Cameron, Harrison *et al.* (2000) *Crossing the Housing and Care Divide*, York: Joseph Rowntree Foundation.

Elderly Accommodation Counsel (2002) *Bringing It All Together*, London: Elderly Accommodation Counsel.

Riseborough, M (1998) *From Consumerism to Citizenship: new European perspectives on independent living in older age*, Oxford: HOPE Network.

Riseborough, M, Fletcher, P and Mullins, D (2001) *The Future of Category One Sheltered Housing*, Birmingham: University of Birmingham and the Housing Corporation.

7 From heritage to vision

How architecture can shape the future living arrangements of older people

Julienne Hanson

Introduction

Written from the standpoint of a practising architect as well as an academic, this paper will consider the part played specifically by architecture in shaping the current repertoire of choices that exists in the UK today, as to where and how to live in later life. The paper is limited to options for living independently (i.e., not residential or nursing care) as these are the circumstances in which some 95 per cent of people find themselves in later life. On the basis of a review and evaluation of the social context and the design precedents for current UK practice, it will be suggested that currently there is not as much choice in third age housing as there appears to be at first sight. Despite the recent emergence of new forms of sheltered and retirement housing in both the public and the private sectors, such as extra care housing and assisted living, a relatively uniform and formulaic design stereotype has dominated the design of sheltered and retirement housing for about the last fifty years. It will be argued that this stereotype, which has admittedly been generated by functional requirements and especially by cost constraints, is nonetheless experienced and perceived by many older people as stigmatising and demeaning. It will therefore be suggested that the rationale that gave rise to the stereotype in the first place, should now be revisited and re-evaluated.

In order to provide a context for re-evaluation, the 'special needs' approach that we have adopted in the UK will be contrasted to more 'inclusive' approaches to the design of people's homes. Design innovations that would seem to be driving change in the foreseeable future will then be highlighted. The paper will conclude by proposing that, for real choice to exist in older people's housing, we need opportunities to make aspirational, lifestyle decisions in later life, not forced moves at times of crisis. In this respect, one of the most significant decisions that increasing numbers of older people will make in the future will be to elect whether to live within a balanced community or as a member of a retirement community. The collective decisions of emerging generations of older people will thus play a major role in shaping the nature, structure and balance of mainstream society in the years to come.

Almshouses, the original 'special needs' housing

The construction of later life as a separate, distinctive lifestage, that of retirement or old-age pensioner, is a relatively recent phenomenon. The average life expectancy at birth in 1901 was 45.5 years for a man and 49 years for a woman (Tinker 1997). The comparable figures today are 75.4 years for a man and 80.2 years for a woman (www.statistics.gov.uk). In 1901, people over retirement age made up just 6 per cent of the total population. By 1951, this figure was 14 per cent and in 2001 people over retirement age accounted for 18 per cent of the total population (www.statistics.gov.uk). A century ago, the age structure of the population resembled a pyramid, with the majority of children and younger adults at the base and a far smaller proportion of older people at the apex. Today the shape of the UK's population banded by age is that of a beehive, composed of a balanced distribution of the youngest and oldest members of the population at the extremes and a slight bulge in the central, mature age groups.

Yet, though only a small proportion of the population survived to old age, secular almshouses had been established in many parts of the country by the sixteenth century for ex-service men, craft guilds, trades and as individual benefactions. Most adopted an inward looking 'collegiate' plan, with rooms set around a central courtyard accessed through archways, with a chapel or common hall at the focus and a mater's lodging by the gate, see Figure 7.1. The concept of the almshouse drew on an alliance of three mutually interdependent elements for its symbolic power: elaborate architecture, ostentatious charitable

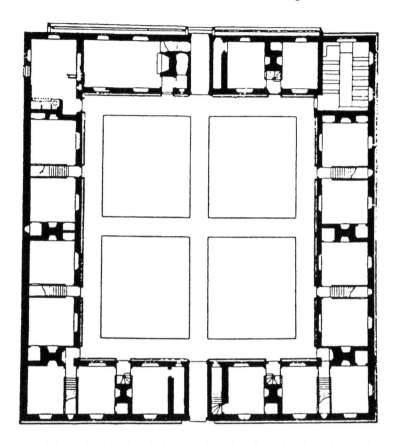

Figure 7.1 Whitgift's Hospital, Croydon, London, 1596, redrawn from Howson, 1993.

giving, and a strong moral message. Though its ultimate beneficiaries were the poor, its originators and financiers were drawn from within a powerful social elite. Fisk (1999) has therefore described the almshouse stereotype as the physical expression of benevolent paternalism, in that the residents 'were the recipients of the beneficence of the aristocracy', p.15.

This 'almshouse stereotype' seems to have exerted a disproportionate effect on the architectural imagination to the numbers housed. Many sheltered and retirement schemes still adopt the elementary spatial gesture of enclosure to represent, in architectural form, a community ethos, simultaneously turning away from (or one's back to) the wider society that lies beyond the gates.

Ordinary mainstream housing

However, up until the second half of the last century, architecture did not impact on the housing circumstances of the vast majority of the population, including older people who lived in ordinary mainstream housing. The UK's general housing stock was – and still is – a mixture of large, medium and small (mainly Victorian) terraced houses and (mainly inter war) solid, well constructed, semi-detached houses, leavened with a smattering of balcony access council flats in city centres. Most of these dwellings were built by speculative builders for sale or, more often, for rent.

Sanitation in working class homes was limited, most likely an outside wc in a lean-to or a shed at the end of the garden. Most small homes did not have a bathroom. The water supply was limited to a cold tap in the scullery or even a shared rising main in the common yard. Room heating was by open, coal fires that were heavy and dusty to service. These homes did not have fitted carpets or central heating. Kitchens were primitive, with no kitchen units or 'white goods'. The dishes were washed in a deep, ceramic sink, cooking took place on a solid fuel or gas fired range and laundry facilities were limited to a copper boiler, washboard and clothes maiden in the scullery.

The birth of the 'welfare state' coincided with the era of post-war reconstruction and wholesale slum clearance. In the push for mass housing, the watchword was quantity not quality. Lowry (1991) and Ineichen (1993) have both pointed out that the post-war council housing building boom produced a generation of unhealthy homes. State sector house building was dominated by an architecture of high rise, high density, system building that produced a new urban landscape of towers, slabs and 'streets in the air'. These have now become modern slums, an icon for the 'failure' of modern architecture. Innovative and largely unpopular architectural solutions to affordable housing have therefore also exerted an influence on the public psyche that is far in excess of their numerical presence as a proportion (1.6 per cent) of the national housing stock (DETR 1998).

The emergence of 'special needs' housing

The dilemma of 'quantity versus quality' applied equally to the provision of post-war council housing and to the contemporary homes that were designed especially for older people whose family were no longer living at home. Under-occupation of family homes by older people led to concerns that the stock of 'general needs' social housing was not being utilised as efficiently as possible. One result was the emergence of 'special needs' during the 1950s, with older people defined as the first and numerically the largest 'special needs' group. A raft of new legislation was passed to put in place the mechanisms that would ensure that older people would not be excluded from rising standards of living. Part III of the National Assistance Act (1948) led to the building of local authority residential care homes and the Housing Act (1957), and 'Flatlets for Older People' (1958) encouraged local authorities to build social rented housing for more independent older people. 'Special Housing' Category I, and 'Sheltered Housing' Category II, were designated in 1969 and new design guidance, 'Housing Standards for the Elderly', became mandatory in all local authorities from June 1970.

This drive to release larger family council homes that were being 'blocked' by retired people and at the same time to make adequate provision for older people moving out of older substandard properties, generated a new form of social housing in the 1960s and 1970s. This was the block of grouped flats and/or flatlets for older people, constructed on one or two floors, with 30 to 50 dwellings to a scheme and net space standards of $30m^2$ for a bedsitting room; $39m^2$ for a one bedroom flatlet; and $44.5m^2$ for a one bedroom flat. Bedsitting rooms were intended for single older occupants and flats/flatlets were designed for occupation by older married couples. Preferred (in effect mandatory) dimensions were set out to guide architects in all aspects of the design of these new 'special' and 'sheltered' housing schemes.

The design stereotypes were developed in a series of experimental housing projects that were widely publicised in the architectural press of the day and were eventually drawn together in 'Housing the Elderly' (1974). The layouts were first published in the 1960s as a result of a sociological study (MHLG 1962) to evaluate the response to 'Flatlets for Older People' (MHLG 1958, 1960), and they were widely adopted by architects designing sheltered housing for local authorities throughout the 1960s and 1970s. The layout appears institutional, and seems to draw for its overall form on the heritage of almshouse architecture. Here, the architecture expresses the 'neediness' of the older

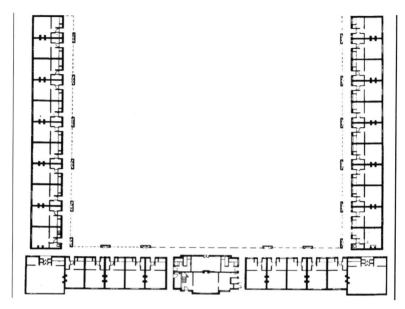

Figure 7.2 A scheme of 32 flatlets that was proposed in 1952 on the edge of a textile town of about 100,000 in south-east Lancashire, redrawn from *Housing the Elderly* (Department of the Environment 1974).

residents and the 'authority' of the welfare state, see Figure 7.2.

People moving into these new flats were expected to be grateful for their smart, modern home and many of those who had moved out of substandard accommodation declared themselves satisfied, despite the drop in space standards that may have accompanied the move. The new flats were designed with modern equipment and fittings that were intended to make older people's everyday lives easier, though concern was expressed at the time that the occupants would not understand or appreciate these technological advances:

> Many old people will have little experience of the latest domestic machinery and, on moving into new homes, they may need advice on how to use it. Without patient and adequate explanation, the accessories of modern living which are meant to help them - central heating systems, safety cookers, baths and showers with safety fittings, washing and drying machines and emergency bell systems - may seem impossibly difficult.
>
> (Department of the Environment 1974, p. 3)

Those who express similar concerns today about older people's resistance to information and communications technologies would do well to reflect on the speed at which the improvements that were made to people's lives during the 1950s became accepted as commonplace and unremarkable.

Trapped in a stigmatising and demeaning stereotype

At the time of its introduction, sheltered housing was a low cost, high volume solution that was more suitable for fit and active elders than for frail older people. The overall layout and the plans of individual dwellings made few concessions to reduced mobility and sensory or cognitive deficits.

The average sheltered housing scheme in England is made up of 25 per cent bedsitting room flatlets like the example show in Figure 7.3, 66 per cent one bedroom flats like the example shown in Figure 7.4 and just 8 per cent are two bedroom dwellings,

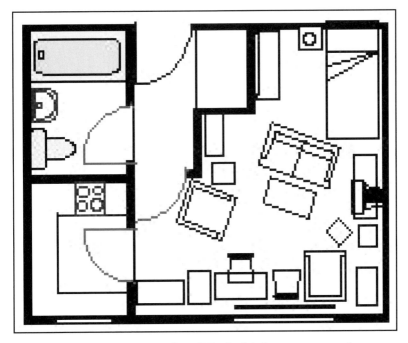

Figure 7.3 Typical example of a 1970s bedsitting room, net floor area 23.71m², reproduced from EPSRC EQUAL research database of over 300 older people's homes, 2001.

though there are significant regional variations. The provision also varies significantly by age, with older 1960s and 1970s sheltered schemes containing a higher proportion of bedsitters and more recent housing a greater proportion of one bedroomed flats (Galvin 1994).

Plan analysis (EPSRC EQUAL 2001) shows that sheltered housing for older people is smaller than the equivalent provision for younger single people. Most flats and bedsitting rooms are designed for 'open plan' living and most layouts offer little scope to conceal the more intimate sleeping area from social and reception space. There is insufficient space in the main living area for a proper dining table so that most occupants are forced to invest in a drop-leaf table that can be set up at mealtimes. There is not enough space to accommodate the furniture and possessions that have been accumulated over a lifetime. Moving into sheltered housing either precipitates a drastic reduction in the amount of furniture one owns or living with clutter (EPSRC EQUAL 2001).

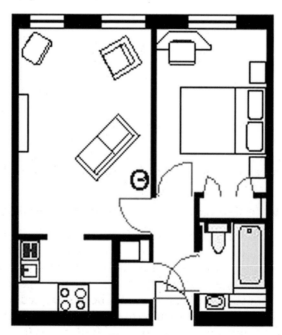

Figure 7.4 Typical example of a 1990s one bedroom flat, net floor are 40.25m^2, reproduced from EPSRC EQUAL research database of over 300 older people's homes, 2001.

Unlike most mainstream homes that have either a kitchen-dining room and a separate living room or a living-dining room and a separate kitchen, in sheltered housing all three functions are compressed into two open plan areas that are connected directly together in a sequence. In more recent examples, the bathroom is connected to the bedroom in a sequence rather like the arrangement that is found between an en suite bathroom and the main bedroom in a family home. Unlike a family home, however, there is no independent family bathroom and so any visitor to the older person's dwelling who wishes to use the toilet must pass through the intimate space of bedroom, which may contain personal or medical items or equipment that the older person might not wish every visitor to see. There is no space in the occupant's personal domain to put-up an overnight visitor, as they are usually catered for in a central guest room that serves the whole complex, or to host a gathering. There is no room to accommodate hobbies and pastimes that require space. In short, sheltered accommodation is designed for living as a couple or alone, not for living independently or interdependently with others.

It is not just that architecture gave an overall form to purpose-designed 'special' and 'sheltered' housing for older people. With the best of intentions, for purely pragmatic reasons, the originators of sheltered housing also invented a 'special' housing stereotype that is unique to older people's housing and that embodies a specific and unflattering view of what it is like to be old. The rationale was 'scientific'. Older people themselves were not consulted. It is a mass, welfare state housing solution. In the choice between quantity and quality, quantity prevailed.

Innovative 'extra care' and 'retirement' housing today

Today, we know most people want to live independently in a mainstream home, and if people opt for purpose-built housing this usually happens at a later stage in life when they are frail and no longer able to look after themselves. The latest generation of 'extra care' housing, see Figure 7.5, has been designed to respond to these changing social requirements. The flat itself has been designed for someone who is older and frailer, and it can usually be adapted for someone in a wheelchair. The common areas in 'extra care' housing schemes are wide, well lit, and easy to negotiate, with a lift to the upper floors. The common facilities

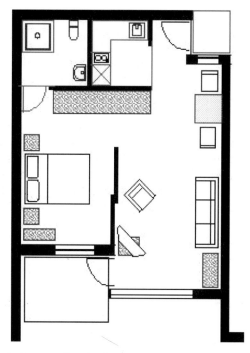

Figure 7.5 Typical example of a late 1990s extra care flat, net floor area 47.87m², reproduced from EPSRC EQUAL research database of over 300 older people's homes, 2001.

are more extensive and may include a restaurant in which a mid-day meal may be provided for residents, and there will be a large, well-appointed hotel-style sitting room. There is usually access on site to services like a local shop, hairdresser and chiropodist. In recognition of the higher support needs of residents, extra care housing also has a high staff–resident ratio and a resident or non-resident manager on the site. Care packages may be arranged and staff may be on call for twenty-four hours a day.

However, analysis of typical extra care layouts confirm that, thirty years on, the smallest flatlets are still a minute 20m², though the average flat size is now a little larger than that of sheltered housing (44 as opposed to 39m²) and a separate bedroom is more common. Two bedroom flats are rare and the plans are still variants on the original 'sheltered' housing stereotype. Note that in the illustrative example shown, the access to the bathroom passes directly through the bedroom.

Recent private sector housing initiatives (usually for sale) that target younger, more affluent older people comprises a wide range of bungalows, flats and apartments to suit older owner occupiers who want to 'downsize' to a smaller home, thus releasing equity bound up in the family home. These schemes are usually designed with the help of an architect. Some are modelled on USA style retirement villages and assisted living communities or occupy prime sites in fashionable coastal resorts. Others hark back to the past and are set in converted heritage properties in the centre of smaller, historic market towns or in large country estates. The concepts that drive retirement housing would seem to include self-segregation, commitment to a 'community of interest' and celebration of an affluent, middle class lifestyle.

The current generation of retirement schemes therefore offer high levels of amenity, yet some – though not all – have adopted a basic flat plan that is identical to the 'sheltered' housing stereotype. In retirement schemes, the average size may be more generous, averaging at about 60m^2, and the architectural style may be more grandiose and flamboyant

Spatial compression

The practical consequence of this impoverished, design-led view of later life therefore affects people in all forms of tenure. Design guidance names about five different types of living room furniture that need to be accommodated in an older person's living room. Room inventories of the living rooms of sixty older people living in a wide variety of housing circumstances from large family houses to a room in a nursing home (EPSRC EQUAL 2001) identified fifty different types of furniture. Guidance suggests that between eight and ten individual items of furniture need to be accommodated in the average living room. The average number of items we observed in the living rooms in our sample was seventeen.

Today, a typical older person's living room inventory might look rather as follows:

- two or three upright chairs, usually part of a dismembered dining room suite;

- two or three easy chairs, which may include part or all of a matching three piece suite and/or a specially purchased 'comfy' chair in which the occupant spends most of the day;

- two low storage units such as a sideboard, cupboard or display case;

- one high storage unit such as a tallboy, shelving, dresser or display cabinet;

- an item of occasional furniture such as a drop-leaf table, side table, telephone table or chest;

- a 'knick knack' such as a plant stand, needlework box or pouffe;

- a standard lamp for accent lighting;

- the TV;

- one or two room heaters, usually to provide a source of radiant heat to 'top up' or replace the central heating; and

- depending on whether or not the room is also used for sleeping, a single bed.

People have to compress their possessions or dismember their home when they move into sheltered housing. This is not just a consequence of today's higher standard of living, as some people in the sample who described to us the process by which they had divested themselves of their possessions, had moved into their home in the 1970s when it was new.

It is equally clear from people's testimonies that many resist the implications of the stereotype by continuing to construct meaningful and detailed environments that reflect their complex social lives. Informants also made observations on what they perceived as the insensitivity of designers:

> *I also feel that architects should be made to live in the houses they design for at least ten years before they put them to the public ... because I think there'd be a lot of changes.*
>
> (Mr T., EPSRC EQUAL 2001)

on the unsuitability of sheltered housing for people who entertain: –

> *It's a one bedroom flat see. I think it's silly really, because when they're making flats for elderly people they should do two bedrooms, because they know they've got families. And they want to come and stay.*
>
> (Mrs F., EPSRC EQUAL 2001)

and on the inadequacy of space standards:

I wonder why it is that they think because you are older you only need enough space to stand up, lie down and sit to eat? That's the impression it gives me! As long as you can sit down somewhere, you can lie down somewhere else and sit down to eat, you don't need anything else. And therefore the space is very confined, very small. The ceilings are low, the rooms are small, the kitchen, you couldn't swing a cat around it. Because you don't cook any more, do you? And you never entertain! So what do you want a kitchen for? You know, that's the thinking behind it!

(Mrs B., EPSRC EQUAL 2001)

Similar criticisms were voiced many times. These are the opinions of a stoical and uncomplaining generation, many of whom had lived through the blitz and all of whom had witnessed a world war. The cohorts of older people who were born during the post war 'baby boom' and in the 'swinging sixties' are likely to have a higher level of material culture and to demand higher space standards, yet this trend has yet to impact on the size and layout of the homes that are being built right now with an anticipated design life of at least thirty years.

One size fits all

It has been proposed that the apparent choice in living arrangements for older people today is largely illusory. The literature on ageing assumes a progressive path from living independently to being cared for. The route is perceived to be marked by actual moves from a mainstream home to some form of purpose-designed (special needs) housing and then on into a residential care home. Design guidance endorses these views by assuming that, once older people move into purpose-built accommodation, they need lower space standards and simple, stereotyped and unimaginative layouts. Architects are not encouraged to explore alternative forms of living arrangements that may better suit the heterogeneous needs and preferences of older people.

Meanwhile, for the 90 per cent of older people who do not live in special housing but in the largely unregulated 'speculative' owner occupied mainstream housing sector, the prospects are not rosy. Despite the recent growth in new homes, the UK housing stock is itself ageing: 45 per cent of homes are over 50 years old, 25 per cent were built before WWI (DETR/EHCS 1998). Statistically, older people are more likely to live in poor housing. Most ordinary family homes have not been designed to cope with poor mobility, physical frailty, sensory loss or cognitive decline, and the new Part M extension of the access requirements in the Building Regulations to new homes, does not go far enough in ensuring that the homes that are currently being built will be fully accessible to persons with reduced mobility.

Homes designed for fit adults are ill-suited to older people's needs and poor design of the built environment can be every bit as disabling as a medical condition. To distinguish this from a medical disability, one might label the adverse effects of poor design as architectural disability.

> Architectural disability occurs when the physical design, layout and construction of buildings and places confronts people with hazards and barriers that make the built environment inconvenient, uncomfortable or unsafe for everyone to use and may even prevent some people from using it at all.
>
> (Hanson 2001, p. 35)

Currently many mainstream homes disable their older occupants. Some actually evict their occupants because they are so disabling, though it would be unfair to blame architects in this case as most mainstream homes were not designed by an architect.

People like to think of their homes as safe places, but most accidents happen at home. Falls by older people accounted for 1752 deaths (1995 data) and 1,047,000 non fatal cases (1996 data); that is, nearly half of all the accidents in each category (HASS 1999). Older people's perceptions of environmental pressure that their home may place upon them and of their increased vulnerability due to living in poor housing therefore accord well with the very real risk they run of suffering an accidental injury or fatal accident at home. People in their eighties and nineties are particularly susceptible to accidents in the home, but these are also problems that affect us all: 90 per cent of people suffer from an 'architectural disability' at some time in their lives. Perhaps it is time to change the paradigm of design culture from one that starts by stating 'what people need' to one that is based on 'user-centred' design, see Figure 7.6.

The seeds of change that indicate change may be on the way can be detected in the 'Lifetime Homes' approach to housing. Launched by the Helen Hamlyn Institute and the Joseph Rowntree Foundation in the late 1980s, this is an assertively

Special Needs	Inclusive Design
Designer-client. Persona of a young, fit, active, white adult, the yardstick for good design	User-clients. People are individuals, who have different needs during their lifecourse
Others – older people and people with disabilities – are not 'normal' clients	Us – we have aspirations as well as problems, older people are 'our future selves'
They have 'special needs'	**We** share 'generic needs'
Ethos of specialisation and pragmatism	Ethos of normalisation and enablement
Tailors the home so it is just right for each client group	Extends parameters of design until no one is excluded
Telling people what they need	Asking people what they want

Figure 7.6 Contrasting design approaches of 'special needs' and 'inclusive design'.

inclusive campaign for accessible mainstream housing, not 'special needs' housing. The movement proposes that all homes can be designed to cope with exigencies of life by improved design in five key areas:

- approach and access
- moving about indoors
- moving between levels
- easy toileting and bathing
- easy environmental control

A design checklist containing recommendations on sixteen features provides a starting point for design.

The underpinning proposition of a Lifetime Home is that no one need be a victim of architectural disability or environmental pressure in their own home, including when one is pregnant, looking after a baby in a pram or a toddler in a pushchair, raising a family, recovering from an accident, entertaining grandparents, having a disabled guest to visit or stay overnight or simply growing older. However the idea behind a Lifetime Home is not that people should actually stay put in their home for the whole of life but rather that it is a home that one can move to without worrying about whether or not it will still be suitable as needs and circumstances change.

A Lifetime Home is an inclusive, mainstream home that should suit most people. It is also trans-generational, in that its principles have been validated by the voices of older people (EPSRC EQUAL 2001) as what they require from a more convenient mainstream home. If *everyone* adopted this approach there would be no need for 'special' housing for any group. Everyone could live how and where they want. The core design principles of Lifetime Homes have already been embraced by 'social' housing providers but not by private house builders. This perpetuates a divisive, micro approach, but for once the social sector benefits from higher standards whilst the mainstream lags behind. Meanwhile, the new generation of up-market private retirement housing and 'gated communities' could make for an even more divided and fragmented society in years to come.

Offering genuine choice

There are those who believe that as standards of living rise, more people own their homes and people age more actively, there will be no need for any purpose-built third age housing at all, especially if everyone will be enabled through higher design standards to live in the mainstream, which is what most older people say they prefer. On the other hand, it is likely that even if all homes were designed using inclusive principles, some people will continue to choose to live in a community of interest. This is because design factors are not the only reason why people elect to live in an age-specific community. Safety and security, support and service, companionship, reduced worries about repairs, gardening and home maintenance are all reasons older people give for choosing to live with their peers. Denying people this option is in itself ageist and stereotyping. Lifetime Homes may widen choice in living arrangements, but they are not a universal panacea.

But for *genuine* choice to exist in how and where to live in later life, we also need to challenge the stereotypes we have inherited from the welfare state in order to make purpose-built housing supportive of people's authentic lifestyle choices.

Continuing to care – for self, home, possessions, other

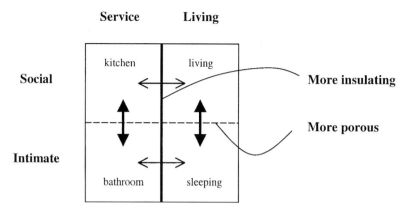

Figure 7.7 A schematic diagram of the underlying sociological dimensions of home.

people – rather than becoming the object of care remains central to maintaining social worth in later life. These aspirations translate into requirements that tend to be strongly social, about having enough space to entertain, share a meal, invite people to stay and engage in hobbies. Other lifestyle factors relate to how one preserves the social niceties, particularly between 'public' and 'private' areas of the home. One thing is clear: a well-designed home can support older people in realising their aspirations whilst a poorly-designed home can frustrate them. The EPSRC EQUAL research (2001) concluded that people of all ages need sufficient space to distinguish service from living areas and social from intimate activities, but in a flexible layout that allows negotiation across the social–intimate and service–living boundaries, see Figure 7.7. Most older people today believe that a 'decent' home requires two public rooms and two private rooms, or at least three rooms that can be used flexibly. On the living side of the diagram, the third room might be a (social) dining room or hobbies room, or on the more intimate side of the equation, it might function as a spare bedroom or room for a carer. On the service side of the diagram, the home might have a larger, more social, kitchen or kitchen-dining room or more space might be invested in a larger bathroom as opposed to a shower room. A flexibly designed home that is able to permutate these possibilities, would allow greater personal freedom to exist than is currently permitted by the current sheltered stereotype.

Technically, it is possible to achieve this degree of flexibility using modern methods of construction. The major obstacles are an unwillingness to experiment or to commit resources to developing alternatives to the 'tried and tested' solutions.

So far as the existing housing stock is concerned, to foster intergenerational integration in balanced communities, up to 20 million older UK homes will need retrofitting if the bulk of the housing stock is to aspire to the Lifetime Homes specification. Existing and new housing will need to be future-proofed to ensure that they incorporate attractive, affordable, road-tested design solutions and products that make everyday living easier, improve quality of life and extend independence in later life. We also need to develop a new, user-centred approach to third age homes that reflects people's aspirations for themselves and their families and friends.

However, inclusive and emancipatory housing design is only the first step. We also need:

● more inclusive transport, access to information, services and public buildings – in short, 'inclusive cities';

● more inclusive forms of tenure – from 'owners and renters' to 'flexible tenure'; and

● an integrated, affordable strategy for the delivery of housing, health and care.

The bottom line is therefore, 'How can we afford it?' Instead of having to chose either quality or quantity as a housing strategy, can we afford both and is this a more sustainable policy for the future?

Inclusive design is cost-effective

The 'special needs' approach has led to a remedial, problem-solving approach where we design for a fragmented customer marketplace, with a consequent low take up of products. This includes 'care homes' and, increasingly, 'sheltered housing'. Design for ageing generally is epitomised by the invention that nobody wants to market, the so-called 'orphan product'. Orphan products are unpopular with mass-market manufacturers because they combine extreme technology with a limited market share and poorly-developed distribution systems.

The 'special needs' approach has also led to unattractive, stigmatising, remedial aids and products. Many are ugly to look at and have been developed from medical products that announce that their user has a disability. Older people are not technophobes, but they do still have aspirations and so products that are unattractive and unstylish tend to be unacceptable to potential users.

So far as housing is concerned, the 'special needs' approach has led to a uniform, unimaginative stereotype that occurs across all tenures and price-brackets. Emerging new constituencies of older people are likely to have exacting standards and to demand 'sexy' products. However, as older people become a larger proportion of the customer base, they could actually be in the vanguard for good design, including that for better-designed housing.

Amongst the more innovative aspirational products that will increasingly be taken up by the mainstream, are emerging information and communications technologies (ICTs) that are already being introduced to the popular housing market through the concept of a 'smart home'. ICTs could be particularly beneficial to older people. Intelligent sensing devices already exist to create an interactive house that can:

- monitor and secure the internal environment;

- provide a passive (automatic) social alarm;

- offer continuous lifestyle monitoring;

- give analysis and feedback on day to day domestic processes; and

- predict and prevent accidents in the home.

Many demonstration projects already exist, but not yet a mass market. New forms of ubiquitous computing – 'chips with everything'– should mean that the technology will be embedded in most household objects in ways that are inconspicuous to their users within the next ten years. As applications increase and the numbers of objects that incorporate a smart interface rise, the price will fall and the technology will become relatively simple and inexpensive to install, thus making it affordable by older people.

More specifically, developments in the field of telecare and telemedicine are confronting the health, support and care interface with home in new and exciting ways. Telecare/medicine involves the delivery of medical services directly into people's homes. The technology can provide everything from a remote diagnosis of symptoms, verbally described, to home monitoring of long term health conditions and the transmission of images and medical data from home to the doctor's surgery or hospital. The idea would not be to replace home care services with machines but to augment human resources in order to release people from routine tasks and allow them to concentrate on delivering high quality, expert care and social contact.

Products of imagination and vision at the cutting edge of design, that should appeal to trend-setters and 'fashion gurus' but that might also benefit older people, include:

- Personal data assistant
- Attentive butler
- Robotic nursing assistant
- Artificial physiotherapist
- Artificial neural networks

Universal appeal is the essential ingredient in broadening the market for these kinds of product (Gans *et al.* 1999).

From welfare provision to mass customisation

The best way to ensure that older people are able to afford, benefit from and desire the emerging home technologies is by making homes and products more attractive, generic and better designed for everyone. However, for this to succeed design has to become user-centred; that is, not ostensibly tailored by designers to suit the perceived needs of older people but genuinely tailored to respond to the diversity of people's real living arrangements and social preferences.

Embracing this inclusive, trans-generational approach to the design of people's living arrangements is therefore not just another formula for standardisation or homogeneity. We must respect gender, ethnicity and consumer identity by customising our future homes and products to make them accessible, available, affordable, appropriate and aspirational. Housing for people of all ages should reflect, not constrain, the diverse lifestyles and values that are characteristic of contemporary society. This is the design challenge that could bring flexible, innovative architecture to the fore in the provision of all types of housing in the years to come.

References

Department of the Environment (1974) *Housing the Elderly*, Lancaster: MTP Construction, p. 222.

DETR (1998) *English House Condition Survey (EHCS): 1996*, London: Department of Environment, Transport and the Regions, p.13.

EPSRC EQUAL (2001) Hanson, J, Kellaher, L and Rowlands, M, *Profiling the Housing Stock for Older People: the transition from domesticity to caring*, Final Report of EPSRC EQUAL Research, University College London.

Fisk, M (1999) *Our Future Home: housing and the inclusion of older people in 2025*, London: Help the Aged, p.15.

Galvin, J (ed.) (1994) *Sheltered Housing in England: an overview of provision*, London: Elderly Accommodation Council, p. 5.

Gans, D, Barlow, J and Venables, T (1999) *Digital Futures: making home smarter*, York: Joseph Rowntree Foundation /Chartered Institute of Housing, p. 60.

Hanson, J (2001) From sheltered housing to lifetime homes: an inclusive approach to housing, Chapter 3 in S Winters (ed.) *Lifetime Housing in Europe*, Hoger institut voor de abeid, Leuven, p. 35.

HASS (1999) *Home Accident Surveillance System Including Leisure Activities*, 21st Annual Report 1997 Data, DTI Government Consumer Accident Data and Safety Research, London.

Howson, B (1993) *Houses of Noble Poverty: a history of the English almshouse*, Sunbury-on-Thames, Middlesex: Belvue Books, p. 92.

Ineichen, B (1993) *Homes and Health: how housing and health interact*, London: E&FN Spon, p. 21.

Lowry, S (1991) *Housing and Health*, London: British Medical Journal.

Ministry of Housing and Local Government (MHLG) (1958) *Flatlets for Older People*, London: HMSO.

Ministry of Housing and Local Government (MHLG) (1960) *More Flatlets for Older People*, London: HMSO.

Ministry of Housing and Local Government (MHLG) (1962) *Grouped Flatlets for Older People: a sociological study*, Design Bulletin 2, London: HMSO.

Tinker, A (1997) *Older People in Modern Society*, 4th edn, London: Longman, p. 13.

COMMENTARY 1

Judith Torrington

Older people inhabit a wide range of settings. The majority live in mainstream housing among the wider community. Of these about a third prefer moving out of family houses to smaller homes such as bungalows or purpose-built flats. Around half a million households in the community receive some home help or care support from external agencies. The remaining 10 per cent of older people live in accommodation catering especially for their needs, spread evenly between sheltered housing and registered care homes (DETR/DH 2001). Architect's engagement in the production of mainstream private housing in the UK is intermittent, but they are much more likely to be involved in publicly funded housing and the production of specialist units catering for distinct populations, and much of the sheltered housing and residential care building stock is architect designed. Writing as an architect it would be good to report that the profession can take pride in the legacy of twentieth-century buildings for the old. There are indeed some fine examples of the genre, but at the same time there are far too many failures. Dissatisfaction with the built environment ranges from criticisms of bland and boring buildings to serious concern about mean spatial provision with inadequate facilities. At the extreme there are unacceptably large numbers of perfectly sound buildings which have been or are about to be demolished because they are not considered fit for the purpose for which they were designed not many years ago. These are the hard-to-let sheltered housing schemes and some of the former local authority homes, characteristically built to high specifications in terms of the building fabric, but with space standards so low that they are now considered intolerable. I wish to identify some of the reasons for past building failures and to suggest strategies that designers might adopt to ensure that the replacement building stock is more future proof and sustainable. I will describe some of the findings from a research project carried out in Sheffield into residential buildings for older people and the implications these may have for design.

What are the reasons for the continued poor performance of older people's housing? There is no single explanation. The buildings that have proved to be unsustainable were not the result of a perfunctory procurement process. Most of them were carefully designed and specified, and conformed to design guidance that was the accepted currency at the time. Failures can be attributed to a range of causes, including historic precedent, poor design guidance, and an over medicalised approach. Predominantly what has changed is the paradigm shift that has repositioned the passive role assigned to old people as the recipients of special housing or care to active empowerment, and this recasting affects everything from the language to the built environment.

Building for quality of life

The importance of lifestyle has been recognised in national research programmes such as the EPSRC EQUAL initiative. The programme is founded on the belief that 'by achieving greater independence and improving the degree of inclusion in all activities of society, older people and disabled people can experience significant improvement in quality of life'. Design in Caring Environments (DICE) is a multidisciplinary research project funded under the EQUAL programme currently being undertaken in Sheffield (Barnes *et al.* 2001). It explores the relationship between the building environment provided by care homes for older people and the quality of life of the building users. The study looked at 35 homes of all types in Sheffield and Rotherham, and about 400 randomly selected residents. Features of the buildings were analysed to find if they had any measurable impact on the quality of the life of the residents. It should be emphasised that the population in residential care necessarily consists of very frail old people. Yet, even in this population, initial findings from the project tend to reinforce the view that active engagement in community life, independence and autonomy give people more fulfilling lives. The aspects of the buildings that correlated best with good quality of life were these:

- the degree of community involvement supported by the building design

- location of the building

- awareness of the outside world

- support for physical disabilities

Conversely high levels of safety provision in the buildings had a negative correlation with quality of life. The implications for design of the findings of this research are significant, particularly when they run counter to what has been accepted practice. They are these:

1 Buildings for older people should invite engagement with the wider community. Traditional and current practice frequently

produces buildings that do the opposite of this. Almshouses were often planned around a secluded courtyard, and recent sheltered housing developments are normally isolated and fortress-like in form.

2 Location of buildings within an active community is preferred. Buildings located in villages and outer suburbs offered better quality of life to their residents.

3 Buildings should maintain awareness of the outside world. A common consequence of ageing is reduced mobility, and a curtailment of activity. More time is spent indoors, so it is important that buildings do not cut people off too much from the normal experience of the world. Conflicts arise between the needs to provide safe, secure, thermally controlled environments and those that communicate changing diurnal and seasonal rhythms and views of outside activity.

4 Good support for physical disability is self-evidently beneficial. A therapeutic environment is one that gives people more choice and control, in contrast with one that is in itself disabling.

5 The conflict between providing a safe environment and a fulfilling one is a major challenge for designers. Clearly buildings need to be safe but it is also true that where there is no risk there is no quality of life. The pressures on providers and administrators of buildings where old people are housed are overwhelmingly on the side of eradicating risk where possible. A clear finding from the DICE study was that buildings frequently have features that are not made use of, for example courtyard gardens that are made inaccessible because they are perceived by staff as possibly hazardous. This attitude leads to buildings where residents are locked up in upstairs corridors with no access to the outside world. Their 'crime' is that they suffer from dementia, and their punishment is a life sentence. Sensitive design strategies combined with informed risk assessment techniques are always preferable to over restriction. Where there is a need to contain wandering residents the best practice is to make the domain available to the individual as big as possible, including some outside space. A gated garden is a better option than a gated corridor.

The legacy of precedent

The three basic types of housing provision have produced a number of variations in response to increasing numbers of older people in the population. The table gives an indication of the range of provision within each type

Mainstream housing	Sheltered housing	Communal homes
Owner occupied houses	Sheltered housing	Residential care homes
Private rented housing	Very sheltered housing	Nursing homes
Social rented housing	Extra care housing	Specialist homes (EMI)
Bungalows	Care villages	
Purpose built flats		
Co-housing		

Sheltered housing and residential care homes inherit differing genealogies. The roots of sheltered housing can be traced to the almshouses of the Middle Ages, and a less palatable line of descent links the communal residential home back to the workhouses of the nineteenth and early twentieth century. Some of the architectural infelicities of both typologies are very persistent and find expression in new buildings. Almshouses characteristically provided individual apartments with very small rooms, minimal provision for cooking and washing in elegant and expensively detailed buildings, with the benefactor's name prominently displayed on the facade. Workhouses, particularly after the Poor Law Amendment Act of 1834, were places where both the architecture and the regime were designed to deter people from wanting to go there, a notoriously successful policy. The abolition of the workhouses in 1930 led to many being taken over and run by local authorities, often for the accommodation of impoverished old people. The dread and fear of the workhouse still persists in folk memory, yet the architectural form resonates with the modern nursing home in detail as well as in overall appearance in, for example, the communal day room and dining hall and the supervised bathing arrangements.

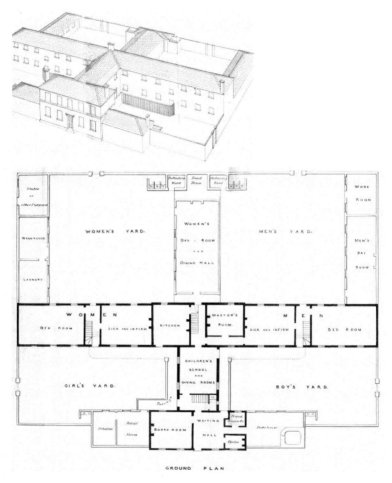

Plan and perspective drawing of nineteenth century workhouse.

Design guidance

A persistent feature of all types of accommodation designed for older people has been the adoption of unacceptably low space standards. This has led to the closure and redundancy of relatively new buildings. It is a curious practice considering the problems associated with restricted mobility and need for access for carers, not to mention the need to accommodate the accumulated possessions of a lifetime. There continues to be a reluctance to build to space standards that can be described as adequate. The new minimum standard of $12m^2$ for a single room in a residential home is not generous, and is well below what is considered adequate in comparable European countries. Space standards in sheltered housing are similarly low, in both public and private sectors. Guidance that advocates that people should be able to have accessible, personalised living space is impossible to achieve within the restricted space provided in much new accommodation.

There is no shortage of design guidance, indeed the architect is faced with an overwhelming amount of data to assimilate and encapsulate in built form. The existence of so much precedent can in itself cause a problem, in that past practice is uncritically passed on into future projects, as sometimes happens when the feasibility of a new development is being assessed. Feasibility proposals are necessarily based on readily available data, particularly in relation to space standards. Project budgets are set on the basis of this information, and the close relationship between building area, cost and number of units provided is the driver of project viability. Once the building area and number of units of accommodation are set there is very little scope for reconsideration, even if further exploration of the design reveals problems. An example of misleading data can be found in the *Homes for old people* section of the Metric Handbook the 'essential boardside reference' to planning data for architects. Typical private room layouts showing bedrooms of 2.4m x 4.00m ($9.6m^{2)}$ and 3.15m x 3.00m ($9.45m^2$) are still being illustrated in the 1999 (latest available) edition, the illustrated rooms contain a single bed, a bedside cabinet and a small chest of drawers. There is the option of either having an armchair or a wheelchair. The wardrobe and the wash hand basin are built in and it is apparent from the drawings that there is room for no other furniture. There is no shelving.

Regulatory standards

While older people in all states of physical and mental health inhabit a range of settings there are considerable differences in the regulatory and statutory standards that apply to different building types. Mainstream housing and sheltered housing need to comply with Building Regulations. Residential care buildings must comply with the National Minimum Standards (Department of Health 2002). There is increasing pressure for innovative building types that inhabit an ill defined area between sheltered housing and full residential care provision to comply with the minimum care standards.

It is incontrovertible that buildings and services provided for vulnerable people should be subject to regulatory control; indeed, much of the legislation springs from a need to eliminate unacceptably low standards of provision that were being offered in the past. The standards cover a range of issues to ensure the physical comfort, accessibility, health and safety, and level of space provision are of a minimum standard. Standards have a powerful effect on raising the base level of provision. However over-regulation can seriously inhibit design quality, leading to the production of bland and unstimulating buildings. The built form that results from uncritical compliance with standards tends to a very uniform environment, and it is a challenge for designers to compensate for these effects. Common problems are:

- double-bank corridors without external reference points producing uniform environments in which people get lost;

- wide-span buildings with poor day lighting in deep plan rooms;

- lack of variation between day and night; permanently lit corridors mean that the building never goes dark at night;

- lack of access to outside space, particularly in buildings organised with discrete units on upper floors;

- uniform year-round temperature;

- lack of natural ventilation;

- circulation areas broken up into discrete sections by fire doors, making navigation difficult;

- medicalised bathrooms and toilets;

- the barring of residents from areas where the normal activities of daily life such as cooking and clothes laundry take place;

- lack of tactile and sensory stimulation of hygienic surfaces and materials.

This is not simply an aesthetic issue. For people who necessarily spend a very high proportion of their time or all of it in one place the design of that space is critical. The potential is for the space to compensate for the inevitable curtailment of activity, and to assist people who for physical or mental reasons are being cut off from the natural world. In practice the spaces designed for old people are too often sterile and boring.

For the architect engaged in design for older people the briefing process gives a strong message that building users have a great number of physical and possible cognitive impairments, and need to live in highly protected environments. While this is often the case it can have a stigmatising effect, and can lead designers to think of the service users as highly problematised with specialised needs. This image is of a medical problem, not a person. The process of building procurement tends to reinforce this perception. Briefing teams normally consist of providers and professional specialists. Hands on managers, wardens or carers, are normally not yet appointed at this stage so are seldom represented in the briefing process. It is very rare indeed that the older people who will use the building have any input. So the designer forms no relationship with the service user as a person.

The writer Rumer Godden reflecting on the reasons for her fruitful and successful old age when she was in her nineties wrote: 'Everyone is a house with four rooms – a physical, a mental, an emotional and a spiritual. Most of us live in one room most of the time, but unless we go into each room every day, if only to keep it aired, we are not a complete person.' The tendency is for buildings that are designed for older people to place a strong emphasis on physical needs but make sparse acknowledgement of the mental, emotional and spiritual side of their inhabitants. A finding of the Sheffield DICE study of residential homes was that the conversions scored consistently higher than purpose-built buildings in the 'awareness of the outside world' category. These buildings are typically conversions of large Victorian or Edwardian houses. The implication is that in designing a 'home' for older people some of the qualities that people associate with home get lost. To score highly in this category buildings need to allow easy congress between inside and outside, views of the outside from the main rooms and circulation spaces, and an ability to perceive changing diurnal and seasonal rhythms.

Choice or standardisation?

On the face of it there seems to be a range of different types of accommodation that would suggest that people can make choices as to where they live. In reality the choice available to any one individual is restricted. Most older people (90 per cent) opt to remain living in mainstream housing where they have always lived. Problems with accessibility and difficulties with managing the home can force people to move. The prospect of more homes being built to Lifetime Home standards may in time help more people to stay put, but it is important to recognise that some people move on from preference as well as necessity. The sheltered housing option appeals to people who want more security and freedom from worries about maintaining their home and garden. There is a frequently reported misconception held by older people that sheltered housing offers more support than is actually the case. Most sheltered housing schemes offer the security of a protected single front door, a maintained building, and a call system to operate in emergencies, but not much more, and there has been an uncomfortable gap between the support needs of people in sheltered housing schemes who are becoming frail and needing support but are not frail enough to be assessed as needing residential care. The development of extra care housing and care villages is beginning to address these needs, and can provide flexible support offering personal care or help in the home tailored to the individual's needs.

For the small number of people who live in residential care the option of living independently is not realistic. The assessment process has ensured that there is virtually nobody living in nursing or residential care homes that could manage on their own in the wider community. This population is made up predominantly of people over 85 who are very fragile, or of people with dementia. This is not a group whose difficulties can be 'designed out' in a Lifetime Home. Suggestions that everyone should be able to remain in the wider community are simply not recognising the frailty and support needs of some people in advanced old age. While in general people when asked resist the idea of moving into residential care very strongly, it is also true that recent surveys have found that people find it better than they expected, and the move into a care home is often regarded as a relief.

The move into a residential home tends to be prompted by a

crisis event, and although the principle that individuals should be able to make informed choices about where they go is widely upheld the reality often falls short of this. Choice is becoming more restricted than formerly for a variety of reasons. The funding crisis has led to widespread closure of homes in financial difficulties. In places where there was until recently over-provision of homes, with a range of types from the small converted privately run family businesses through to medium to large homes run by voluntary organisations and local authorities to large purpose built homes for residential or nursing care (or registered for both) run by corporate providers, there may now be significant gaps in provision. The small-scale family-run businesses have come off worst, and many of these have closed. Former local authority (Part Three) homes have now largely been handed over to voluntary trusts. Difficulties in bringing these buildings up to the level required by the National Care Standards, particularly in respect of room sizes have led to widespread closures and modifications in this sector. The regulations themselves have had a unifying effect on care homes with minimum sizes being adopted as a universal size, and a dominant building typology.

Conclusion

Designing for older people should not be an insurmountable challenge. Increasing numbers of older people in the population make it an urgent one. It is both in the interests of individual older people and of society as a whole that in whatever kind of accommodation people are to be housed they should remain as independent as possible, and there is evidence that a supportive built environment can assist this process. People need a wide choice of housing provision. Within that choice there appear to be some universal design principals that apply regardless of the building type. These are:

- building users should be involved in the design process;

- space standards need to be generous;

- buildings for older people should be extrovert rather than introvert in nature, engaging with a wider community;

- buildings should maintain people's ability to feel in contact with the natural world;

- support is needed for physical frailty;
- a reasonable balance should be achieved between safety and security provision and restriction on quality of life.

The aim must be to produce robust building typologies that have an enduring popular appeal. Good models are the bungalow, recently voted the most popular form of housing, and in the collegiate living models developed in Oxford and Cambridge for communal living environments. The hope is that more enduring and sustainable forms of housing for old people can be achieved in the twenty-first century.

References

Barnes, S, McKee, KJ, *et al.* (2001) The design in caring environments study, in S Tester, C Archibald, C Rowlings and S Turner (eds) *Quality in Later Life: rights, rhetoric and reality*. Proceedings of the British Society of Gerontology 30th Annual Conference, Stirling, Scotland: University of Stirling.

DETR/DH (2001) *Quality and Choice for Older People's Housing: a strategic framework*, London: DTLR.

Department of Health (2002) *Care Homes for Older People: National Minimum Standards*, London: Department of Health.

8 Conclusions

Keith Sumner

Key issues

It is not my intention to engage in a lengthy analysis of those questions raised, the arguments proposed and the solutions that have been put forward expertly, and eloquently, by the contributors and examined through the commentary pieces. However, I would like to revisit a small number of the points made throughout the texts. I shall then cast the net a little wider to highlight briefly some of the broader policy structures and frameworks within which housing policy and provision, for older people in particular, is framed.

Gillian Dalley (chapter 2) urges us to dig beneath the surface of the ideology behind 'promoting independence' and recognise it for the double-edged sword that it is. In appearing to support the perceived wishes of the majority, it can be used as a smoke-screen for the neglect, or de-investment of public funds into forms of accommodation and support that are not considered to fit the narrow conception of the meaning of independence. This is most apparent in the current heated debate going on around the future of residential and nursing care homes, where provision in both the state and independent sectors is undergoing change unprecedented in recent times. It is, however, no less true of the problems encountered in trying to realise other forms of communal living, such as co-housing. Maria Brenton (chapter 6) outlines some of the difficulties in working with local authorities to secure public support, and funds, for such ventures.

Crucial to the acceptability of the various options in living arrangements is the task of ensuring that these values of independence and autonomy can be realised whatever the setting. Though this poses particular challenges for residential forms of care it is not beyond the bounds of possibility. The whole arena of communal forms of living is one that suffers from neglect as it is widely perceived as outside the boundaries of prevailing concepts offering the individual the opportunity to maintain their independence, seen as untenable within 'institutional' settings.

In chapter 3, Leonie Kellaher reminds us that older people are far from passive in their attempts to maintain their self-identity and adapt whatever forms of housing they find themselves in to meet their requirements. What is missing is the embracing of the thinking strategies employed by older people, and what motivates them to make the choices that they do, from those that are open to them. Until this is achieved the supply of accommodation will bear only a tenuous link to what older people would be likely to demand. Significant progress is being made to involve older people at all levels of planning and decision making, particularly in the local government arena, including housing decisions, with the 'Better Government for Older People' programme perhaps the best example, but it is still in its infancy and very patchy in implementation. The outcomes of the ongoing study being undertaken by Lancaster University and Counsel and Care, 'Housing Decisions in Old Age' (Clough *et al.*, commenced 2000) should contribute a good deal to our understanding in this area.

Karen Glaser and Cecilia Tomassini (chapter 4) illustrate the complexity of the changing patterns of relationships and household composition amongst older age groups. Linear projections of future need are valuable, but have limitations, as a multiplicity of factors impinge upon patterns of living, with divergent groups growing and declining simultaneously. An example of this is the parallel increase in older people living alone and also that of co-habiting couples. Changes in the patterns of available communal or residential forms of living will further impact on attempts to predict people's future care or support needs based on demographic data modelling projections. The apparent decline of traditional forms of residential provision on the one hand and the growth of innovative forms of communal living, such as co-housing (chapter 6), often with people living separately, but as part of a supportive, co-operative community illustrates this complexity.

There are both dangers and opportunities that may be realised within existing policy frameworks, and with those that are soon to take effect. Isobel Allen's timely reminder, and some of the points raised by Helena Herklots and Kalyani Gandhi (chapter 5) can be considered to emphasise the negative consequences of a government lacking the political will to ensure genuine diversity is supported.

It is clear from the population trends highlighted by Glaser and Tomassini, and the rising expectations of the ageing post-war 'baby-boomers', that many traditional forms of sheltered housing and residential care are increasingly unacceptable in their present form. This is mirrored by the inadequate robustness of support services to enable those who wish to remain in their existing 'mainstream' accommodation such as domiciliary care services and Home Improvement Agencies (partially addressed in the recent housing green paper) in which issues of staff recruitment and retention and adequate long-term funding are key.

The 'Supporting People' initiative paves the way for much more freedom and innovation within the housing and care arena, both in terms of funding and support following the person. However, the cash-limited pots of money that will be available to local authorities and the attendant assessment procedures, raises the prospect of many of the concerns now familiar to us in relation to community care assessments, eligibility criteria and 'rationing' of resources.

Both Julienne Hanson and Judith Torrington (chapter 7) illustrate that at the design and planning stages, 'quality of life' factors can, to a considerable extent, be built into accommodation. The knowledge, skills and technologies to achieve this are already with us (Phippen 2000).

Hanson also echoes other contributors, for example, Malcolm Fisk (chapter 2) in arguing that embracing a trans-generational approach to the design of people's living arrangements, will improve their accessibility, availability and affordability for all, including older people. This is an aspect of a long-standing debate within social gerontology and the broader disability and equalities fields. It centres around segregationalism, at one end of the spectrum, perhaps typified by the growth of large, self-contained retirement communities or villages, and integration at the other, illustrated by the development of 'Lifetime Homes'.

I do not believe that these positions are irreconcilable and tend to concur with the argument put forward by Heywood *et al.* (2002) who advocate housing policies that promote balanced communities. They propose that 'anti-collective living attitudes are dispensed with, in favour of an expansion of living situations chosen by older people, designed by older people and controlled by older people' going on to state that this broadening of options for older people 'by no means undermines the previous plea for more balanced communities' (p.165).

Final remarks

The start of this decade has seen a reversal of long-standing trends in 'real terms' reduction, or over-restraint in the funding of many public sector services. The years 2000 and 2001 saw the amount of money available for housing investment rise significantly. Funding increases to realise the aspirations contained within the NHS Plan are substantial, as were those subsequently contained within the 2002 public spending review. A year which also witnessed the biggest increase in the injection of cash for local authority social services departments for many years. All these are welcome and necessary steps in the right direction, but what is also needed is what Heywood *et al.* (2002) term a new 'mind-set' to combat what they see as the two reasons for neglect, those of money and attitudes. They state 'the most effective method of arriving at a new mind-set, which would influence researchers, policy makers and practitioners, is to involve older people in the policy and practice process' (p.163).

This is a theme running throughout this publication, participation and the empowerment to influence one's own future and the nature of housing and care provision for older people locally and nationally. The proliferation of legislation from the late 1980s onwards, the implementation of the NHS and Community Care Act (1990) and the range of initiatives since the election of a Labour government in 1997 (for example, Health Improvement Programmes, Joint Investment Plans, Better Government for Older People, noted above, and the National Service Frameworks) all emphasise full involvement in decision making around care options at an individual level and strategic involvement in local service development through older people's representation on inter-agency service planning fora.

So, many of the mechanisms to facilitate this influence are in place, but it is increasingly clear that the effectiveness of this representation of older people's views, and how that has translated into real change in local strategic planning is questionable. This is certainly the case across the health and social care spectrum, and even more so within housing services planning.

It is, however, not enough to ensure that this emerging potential is made a reality. Older people's resources to exert such influence needs to be in harness with architects, designers and planners at all stages to enable boundaries to be pushed to their limits. Without such action on this range of fronts it will not be possible to claim real progress towards addressing the needs of the diverse wishes of older people today and in the coming decades. It is hoped that the readership will contribute towards carrying forward the aims of this book and all those who have contributed to it.

References

Brenton, M (1998) *We're In Charge – Co-Housing Communities in the Nederlands: lessons for Britain?* Bristol: Policy Press.

Clough, R, Leamey, M, Miller, V, Bright, L and Brooks, L, Housing Decisions in Old Age, Lancaster University, unpublished, see: http://www.lancs.ac.uk/depts/apsocsci/research/index.htm

Dalley, G (2001) *Owning Independence in Retirement: the role and benefits of private sheltered housing for older people*, London: Centre for Policy on Ageing.

Heywood, F, Oldman, C and Means, R (2002) *Housing and Home In Later Life*, Buckingham: Open University Press.

Phippen, P (2000) *Building for Longevity: Abbeyfield Lecture 2000*, St Albans: Abbeyfield Society.

Appendix

Participants in the seminar series 'Choice in Later Life
Living Arrangements'

Sue Adams – Chief Executive, Care and Repair England
Professor Isobel Allen – Policy Studies Institute
Nigel Appleton – Director, Contact Consulting
Kina, Lady Avebury – Vice Chair of the Board of Governors, Centre for
    Policy on Ageing
Cheryl Barrott – 50+ Group/Elders Congress Officer, Sheffield City
    Council
Professor Graham Beaumont – School of Psychology and Counselling,
    University of Surrey, Roehampton.
Maureen Bell – Regional Manager, Foundations
Professor Miriam Bernard – Centre for Social Gerontology, Keele
    University
Bob Bessel – Chief Executive, Retirement Security Housing
Professor Alison Bowes – University of Stirling
Kathleen Boyle – Consultant/Trainer, Peter Fletcher Associates
Maria Brenton –University of Bristol / Consultant, Joseph Rowntree
    Foundation
Les Bright – Deputy Chief Executive, Counsel and Care
Dr Vanessa Burholt, Deputy Director, Centre for Social Policy Research
    and Development, University of Wales, Bangor
John Burton – Independent Social Care Consultant
Stephanie Canham – Head of Social Care (Adults), Herefordshire
    County Council
Dr Sangeeta Chattoo – Centre for Research in Primary Care, Leeds
    University
Carmel Conefrey – Policy Officer, LGA
Julie Cowans – Housing Research/Development Manager, Joseph
    Rowntree Foundation

Gillian Crosby – Deputy Director, Centre for Policy on Ageing
Janet Dale – Vice Chair, Hartrigg Oaks Residents Committee
Gillian Dalley – Director, Centre for Policy on Ageing
Gary Day – Managing Director, McCarthy & Stone
Aboo Zaid Dowlut – Director of Care and Support Services, ASRA
    Greater London HA
Paul Espley – Head of Housing Policy and Performance, Servite Houses
    Housing Association/EROSH Representative
Maria Evandrou – Senior Lecturer, Age Concern Institute of
    Gerontology, King's College London and Co-Director of SAGE
    (LSE)
Malcolm Fisk – Director, Insight Social Research Ltd
David Fotheringham – Chartered Institute of Housing
John Galvin – Director, Elderly Accommodation Counsel
Kalyani Gandhi – Eastwards Trust Housing Association
David Gardiner – BGOP Older Peoples National Advisory Group
    Member
Cydonie Garfield – Jewish Care Homes Housing Association
John Gatward – Group Chief Executive, Hanover Housing
Dr Karen Glaser – Lecturer, Age Concern Institute of Gerontology,
    King's College London
Martin Green – Chief Executive, Counsel and Care
Dr Julienne Hanson (Architect) – Bartlett School of Graduate Studies,
    UCL
Helena Herklots – Assistant Director, Policy, Age Concern
Ian Ireland – BUPA Care Homes
Lilian James – Bradely Village Retirement Community, Residents Board
    of Directors Representative
Mike Jennings – Operations Director (South), McCarthy & Stone
Alison Johnson – Independent Consultant
Glenys Jones – Chair, Older Peoples Committee, Association of
    Directors of Social Services, and Director, Middlesborough Social
    Services
John Kennedy – Joseph Rowntree Housing Trust (Hartrigg Oaks)
Una Larter – Member of OWCH, the Older Womens CoHousing Group
    (London)
Patrick Manwell – Architect, Archadia
Kathy McEnnerney – Bradely Village Retirement Community,
    Staffordshire Housing Association
Marina Mele – Hsg/SSD Service Manager, Strategic Planning and
    Partnerships, Luton Borough Council
Larry O'Neil – DTLR, Planning Directorate
Anne-Marie Nicholson – Architect, PRP Architects
Dr Christine Oldman – Centre for Housing Policy, York University
Steve Ongeri – Senior Policy Analyst, Housing Corporation
Imogen Parry – Chair, EROSH (Emerging Role of Sheltered Housing)

Dr Sheila Peace – School of Health and Social Welfare, The Open
    University
Dr John Percival – Independent Social Care Consultant
Heather Petch – Director, hact
Peter Phippen – PRP Architects
David Richardson – Director of Welfare, Air Forces Housing Association
Moyra Riseborough – Lecturer, Centre for Urban and Regional Studies
    Birmingham University
Francesca Seymour – Policy Advisor, Housing Care and Support
    Division, DTLR
Jef Smith – Editor, Registered Homes and Services Journal
Keith Sumner – Policy Officer, Centre for Policy on Ageing
Annie Stevenson – Health Policy Manager, Help the Aged
Barbara Swann – The Architecture Studio Ltd
Dr Cecilia Tomassini – Department of Demography, University La
    Sapienza, Rome
Judith Torrington – Architect, Sheffield University
Stephen Townsend MBE – Older Peoples Advisory Group, Better
    Government for Older People programme
Dr Oliver Valins – Institute of Jewish Policy Research
Joan Vessey – Co-Chair, Sheffield BGOP 50+ Group/Elders Congress

Index

Note: Page numbers in *italics* refer to tables.